To my sexually
deviant sister

XOXO

Brother

Useless Sexual Trivia

Tastefully Prurient Facts About Everyone's Favorite Subject

Shane Mooney

A Fireside Book
Published by Simon & Schuster

FIRESIDE
Rockefeller Center
1230 Avenue of the Americas
New York, NY 10020

Designed by Gabriel Levine

Manufactured in the United States of America

10 9 8 7 6 5 4 3 2 1

Library of Congress Cataloging-in-Publication Data
Mooney, Shane.
Useless sexual trivia : tastefully prurient facts about everyone's favorite subject / Shane Mooney.
p. cm.
1. Sex Miscellanea. 2. Sex customs Miscellanea.
I. Title
HQ25 .M65 2000
306.7—dc21 99-41157 CIP
ISBN 0-684-85927-0

To my loving wife, Samantha

And to Jessica: If anyone can make sex trivial, it's her.

Contents

Fore-Play

Did you know that . . .

The word "vanilla" comes from the Latin word vagina, because of the vanilla pod's resemblance to the female genitalia.

In Middle Eastern Islamic countries it is not only a sin, but a crime as well, to eat a lamb that you've had sex with.

The male pig has a corkscrew shaped penis that looks like his tail, and he slowly "winds" into the female pig before achieving a ten-minute-long orgasm.

While the above information hasn't raised your IQ,

helped you to find a high-paying job, or improved your own personal love life, you no doubt find yourself richer for having the knowledge. (At least you've got something to say during those long lulls in the conversation.)

If you're like most people, you have a fascination with sex, otherwise you wouldn't be reading this book. While nearly every magazine from *Cosmo* to *Sports Illustrated*—and even *The Wall Street Journal*—manages to work its fair share of articles on everyone's favorite subject into its pages, the most interesting facts go far beyond your garden-variety coitus. There's a tremendous amount of intriguing material about sex to be found in all areas of life, from animals to history to the rich and famous.

Within these pages I've attempted to gather every little fascinating factoid, titillating tidbit, and carnal curiosity on the world's favorite pastime. And while everyone does indeed enjoy sex and loves to hear more about it, I wanted to make sure that the book could be enjoyed by a wide range of readers. I tried to avoid being raw and overly explicit, choosing instead to be tastefully prurient and use fouler language and more-graphic detail only when absolutely necessary. I think you'll find that this book truly details everything you wanted to know about sex but didn't know to ask. And all of it's guaranteed to be completely useless.

Useless Sexual Trivia

1 Just the Factoids, Man

It's the little sexual factoids that make life, as well as any dull dinner conversation, so interesting. The next time you find yourself at a party discussing the merits of separation of church and state over the guacamole, you can comment that the word "avocado" actually comes from a Nahuatl word meaning "testicle," and then watch the conversation switch into overdrive. With the following factoids, you're sure to be a hit at the next family reunion.

The term "scumbag" originally referred to a used condom.

Menstrual cramps have been known, in rare cases, to induce orgasm.

* * *

For some reason, the more years of formal education, the more wet dreams a man is likely to have.

Women are most likely to want to commit adultery when they're ovulating.

Australian women, according to statistics, are the most likely to have sex on the first date.

The name of Wyoming's Grand Teton peak literally means "big tit."

In the original Grimm's "Sleeping Beauty" fairy tale, the prince rapes her while she sleeps and then leaves before she wakes up.

Most wedding traditions have to do with sex. The purpose of a flower girl as well as unmarried bridesmaids was to increase the sheer abundance of virginity, necessary to ward off demonic forces naturally drawn to such an event. The honking of car horns, the clinking of glasses, and the throwing of rice and other "seeds of life" was to ensure successful—procreative—sex. And the throwing of the bridal bouquet actually symbolized the loss of virginity.

Women who went to college are more likely than high school dropouts to enjoy both the giving and receiving of oral sex.

* * *

Catholic girls were told never to wear patent leather shoes because they would reflect what was up their skirts.

No wonder we think it's evil: the word "masturbation" comes from a Latin word meaning "to pollute oneself."

It's been proven to be harder to tell a convincing lie to someone you find sexually attractive.

However, adults are more likely to tell a lie in bed than anywhere else.

Most men can't remember the names of all their sex partners.

The word "avocado" comes from the Spanish word *aguacate,* which in turn is derived from the Nahuatl word *ahuacatl,* which meant "testicle." You'll probably never look at guacamole the same way again.

In all likelihood, a boy couldn't get a girl pregnant with his first ejaculation, as it takes one to three years afterward for a male's ejaculate to become potent.

A William Shakespeare euphemism for a couple having sex was "making a beast with two backs." He also called the female genitals "charged chambers" and "birds' nests."

* * *

In April 1970, Gloria Sykes won a judgment of $50,000 against San Francisco's transportation system for her injuries sustained in a cable car accident. Her claim wasn't for physical harm like a broken leg, though she did get two black eyes and several bruises. The main crux of her argument revolved around the fact that she was now a nymphomaniac: she once had sex fifty times within a five-day period.

The eyelid and the skin of the scrotum are the only parts of the male body that contain no subcutaneous fat.

It's believed that the purpose of pubic hair is to trap the scents released by the secretions in the pubic region. (Ditto for armpit hair.) For what purpose? Reportedly the secretions serve as an erotic stimulus to the opposite sex.

In eighteenth-century France, a woman named Madame Ventre, who lived in Marseilles, had a fully functioning, lactating breast that stuck out of her left thigh just below the waist.*

The term "venereal disease" was coined in the sixteenth century and originated from the Latin phrase *morbus Veneris,*

*Extra breasts—a condition called "polymastia"—are rare, but not entirely unheard of. In 1886 there were two women who each had ten breasts, all of which secreted milk, and in 1894 there was a case reported of a man who possessed eight breasts.

"the sickness of Venus," goddess of love (which is the euphemistic way of saying goddess of sex).

Semen contains minute quantities of more than thirty elements, such as fructose, ascorbic acid, cholesterol, creatine, citric acid, urea, uric acid, sorbitol, pyruvic acid, glutathione, inositol, lactic acid, nitrogen, vitamin B_{12}, various salts, and enzymes.

In the world of porn, it's the women who make more money, typically $500–$1,000 per film, depending on star power and the acts involved, while men usually earn $500 or less, depending on star power (which, of course, can push the pay for either sex into several thousands).

It's not mere hooey when they say that people *love* chocolate; the same chemical responsible for the ecstatic highs of love and sexual attraction, phenylethylamine, is found also in chocolate.

We use the expression "tenderloin district" because corrupt cops who took bribes from the prostitutes, pimps, and madams of the area could upgrade their diets.

"Buckle bunnies" is the affectionate term given to women who go to rodeos with the express intent of getting sex from one of the cowboys.

* * *

The notorious movie *Deep Throat* cost less than $50,000 to make and has earned more than $100 million, which makes it the most successful porno of all time.

While we think of Cupid today as an innocent youth with bow and arrow, his original representation by the pedophiliac Greeks was that of a beautiful young boy whose naked form was considered to be the embodiment of sexual love.

It was during the sexually repressive Victorian era that the formerly nude Cupid was redesigned as wearing a skirt.

Thanks to the wonders of modern technology, we can now take comfort in knowing, finally, that a male fetus is capable of an erection in the last trimester of gestation.

The word "penis" is Latin for "tail."

Ever wonder what a pap is and why it needs to be smeared? The Pap smear is named after the U.S. pathologist Dr. George N. Papanicolaou.

The labia minora of women who've given birth are darker than those of women who haven't.

Mark Wahlberg has three nipples. The third nipple was airbrushed out of his underwear ads.

Among transsexuals who choose sex-change surgery, females who elect to become male are reported to be happier and better adjusted postoperatively than males who elect to become female.

The *Kama Sutra* details techniques on ten types of kisses, sixty-four different caresses, eight variations on oral sex, and eighty-four positions for intercourse. It's also believed that the author, Mallanga Vatsyayana, was celibate and wrote the book through divine knowledge.

For most women, the libido peaks just before menstruation.

Believe it or not, a survey conducted by Masters and Johnson in the early eighties revealed that heterosexual encounters were the third-most-frequent fantasy of both male and female homosexuals.

Things considered to be sexually deviant behavior, such as fetishism, exhibitionism, and zoophilia, to name a few, are reported to be almost exclusively male.

The word "gymnasium" comes from the Greek word *gymnazein,* which means "to exercise naked."

Sperm banks keep their donor semen at approximately -321 degrees Fahrenheit, and it can be kept indefinitely.

A flasher apparently doesn't get his jollies from sheer exhibitionism. It's the shock of his audience, which he mistakes for sexual excitement, that keeps him going.

Exhibitionists are most likely to be married men.

Alcoholics have AA, drug users have NA, and those unfortunate enough to suffer from compulsive or pathological sexual behavior have somewhere to turn as well, thanks to the 1976 founding of SLAA (Sex and Love Addicts Anonymous), which has a similar twelve-step recovery plan.

The word "fornication" comes from the Latin word *fornix*, meaning "arch." Roman street prostitutes found brisk trade underneath the arches of the Colosseum, servicing male patrons whose passions were aroused by the blood and violence of the games or by an erotically stimulating play.

The usual result of ingesting true Spanish fly is vomiting. While some Romans thought this to be arousing, this is probably not the end result one desires in an aphrodisiac.

The fluffer is the woman who, between takes, helps to ensure a male porn actor's readiness, though with the advent of tight-budgeted, straight-to-video films, fluffers are not as common as they once were. For gay films, there's a fluff boy.

"Fag hag" is the affectionate term given to straight women

who prefer the company of gay men.

The word "negligee" originally came from the Latin *neglegere,* which literally translates as "don't pick up" or "don't clean the house."

According to *Penthouse,* more women complain about infrequent sex than men do.

Still deciding on a major? Consider this: The Kinsey Institute library's film and video collection contains a variety of VHS, Beta, 16 mm, and 8 mm films relating to human sexuality. The historical films (over six thousand reels) are primarily heterosexual commercial erotica dating from 1912 through the 1970s, but among them are also medical films, homosexual erotica, some eighty films documenting mammalian sexual behavior, and a few examples of avant-garde films.

The more contemporary collection consists primarily of VHS and some Beta tapes. These tapes cover six main areas: heterosexual erotica, homosexual male erotica, homosexual female erotica, sex education and therapy, transvestites, and sadomasochism/bondage. There are approximately seven thousand videotapes.

The average man reaches his sexual peak when he's seventeen or eighteen.

* * *

Most women report that they prefer to have sex in the dark.

During cold weather, the body automatically moves the testes closer to the body for warmth in order to keep things environmentally pleasant for the ever-at-the-ready sperm. The reverse happens in warmer weather, for the same reason.

Men become sexually aroused nearly every time they dream.

Thinking about a part-time job? Commercial sperm banks pay screened donors an average of $50 per specimen.

The left testicle usually hangs lower than the right, though, surprisingly, the right testicle has been found to be lower with left-handed men.

Women who are housewives are as a whole more faithful than working women.

If kept in a billfold, a condom usually loses its ability to protect after about a month, due to the body heat breaking the rubber down.

The number of sperm that could be fit into an aspirin capsule would be enough to repopulate the earth to its present numbers.

Readers of *Cosmopolitan* said that they're more turned on by music than by pornography.

For reasons yet to be fully understood, the average sperm count of American men has actually declined since the 1950s.

Women say that the part of a man's body that they admire most is his buttocks.

The number of female ova necessary to repopulate the world could fit into a chicken egg.

Most men produce the most amount of sperm between the ages of twenty and thirty.

Jazz fans, gun owners, and those who lack confidence in the president are among the most sexually active Americans.

A college-educated man is more likely to enjoy sex completely in the nude than a high school graduate.

The most popular sexual aid according to *Playboy* is erotic literature (like they were going to say something else?).

Married men masturbate more often than married women.

Proof that sex is a prerequisite for cervical cancer: devoted nuns never get it.

* * *

As a general rule, men have a tendency to fantasize more about scantily clad women than about those that are naked.

Among primates, man has the largest and thickest penis.

According to *Playboy,* most men feel that the most satisfying moment of intercourse is when their partner climaxes.

According to a recent survey, more Americans lose their virginity in June than in any other month (must be all those proms and weddings).

According to *Playboy,* football is the spectator sport most arousing to women.

It's possible for men to have an erection at the time of death. It was quite common at hangings.

Besides the genitals and the breasts, the inner nose also swells during intercourse.

According to *Playboy,* more men have experienced threesomes than women.

The first issue of *Playboy,* in 1953, which sold for a mere fifty cents, was never dated, because Hugh Hefner assumed that he'd never publish another.

* * *

According to people who keep track of such things, the man is the most likely partner to be tied up during sex.

A survey done by *Playboy* proved that the majority of men find a woman's breasts to be the sexiest part of her body.

Fellatio is the most common form of sexual activity among homosexual men.

The Mayflower Madam once remarked that of all her high-priced call girls, the redheads were the least desired by her clients.

The first "official" vasectomy was performed in 1893.

A small flaccid penis generally has a greater-percentage increase during erection than a larger flaccid penis.

The average age of menopause has increased in the last hundred years from the forties to the fifties.

According to Kinsey, masturbation is more common among white-collar workers than blue-collar workers.

A psychotherapist is the most likely professional to have a sexual affair with his client, though some would argue it's lawyers.

* * *

The vast majority of clients at a house of prostitution are married.

Cosmopolitan magazine says that the vibrator most recommended by sex therapists is the Hitachi Magic Wand.

The frequency with which a woman has orgasms during her sleep actually increases as she ages during her childbearing years.

Prostitution may be legal in Nevada, but only in towns with a population of less than two hundred thousand.

It's normal for a baby to experience an orgasm in the first weeks of life.

A 1975 study confirmed that men are more sexually attracted to women with enlarged *pupils*.

According to *Playboy*, more women talk dirty during sex than men.

Odds are more likely that a single woman will get lucky this weekend than a single man.

Atheists, non-Christians, and Jews tend to be more sexually active than those Americans professing to be practicing

Christians.

White women, and those women with a college degree in particular, are the most receptive to anal sex.

According to statistics, most straight men haven't a clue when their partner is having an orgasm, which is why they usually ask, "Was it good for you?"

2 Sex by the Numbers

Let's face it: sex is a numbers game. Everyone's wanting to know how many times you do it, how much you have, or how much the other person has. Whether you're interested in learning the average size of a penis, how many calories are burned during typical sex (the non-swinging-from-the-chandelier variety), or just plain old sexual statistics, this chapter is for you.

Of the twenty-five reported cases of penis fracture, sixteen of the men agreed that the cause of their condition was overenthusiastic masturbation.*

*While you may ask how it's possible for something without an actual bone to get fractured, rest assured that penile fracture does indeed happen, and in fact, there are even leading experts in

* * *

Every day, 200 million couples around the world have sex, which figures out to over two thousand couples at any given moment.

Going blind is the least of your worries . . . It's estimated by some that the practice of autoerotic asphyxiation (temporarily suffocating yourself while masturbating) takes the lives of 250 to a thousand men and women a year.

Fifty-eight percent of women who've read a *Penthouse* magazine would be willing to have sex with a complete stranger for a million dollars.

Women with a Ph.D. are twice as likely to be interested in a one-night stand than those with only a bachelor's degree.

---

this particular field. The penis, while containing no bone, does get rigid, and things that get rigid can break. The corpora cavernosa, or the parts of the inside that get filled with blood to make a penis erect, get stretched pretty thin; any sudden jolt in the wrong place and you could pop like a balloon (as well as damage your urethra and the outer sheath of your penis). How can you tell when fracture has occurred? Well, the telltale sign is a loud cracking sound, which should be your clue to get to a hospital ASAP. In the old days, treatment usually involved a splint, ice packs, and drugs to suppress erections (kind of anti-Viagra), though to be honest, these treatments usually resulted in permanent disfigurement. Nowadays, repairing the damage surgically is the most common option.

In case the above hasn't encouraged you to be a bit more careful, here's one particular account: "A 26 year-old male . . . experienced sudden acute pain and prompt detumescence during vigorous coital activity. The episode was associated with an audible cracking sound [and] his penis became grossly swollen."

* * *

And now for the moment we've all been waiting for: THE LENGTH OF THE AVERAGE PENIS. Leave it to our friends at the Alfred C. Kinsey Institute for Sex Research to tackle the specifics. In a study of college males, the study cases were given a ruler, sent into a private area, and then told to measure their erect penis from where it met the body (along the top) to the tip. Keep in mind that the measurements were carried out in private, so there may be a bit of exaggeration; these are college men, after all.

Percentage of Men	Length (in Inches)
0.2	3.75
0.3	4
0.2	4.25
1.7	4.5
0.8	4.75
4.2	5
4.4	5.25
10.7	5.5
8	5.75
23.9	**6**
8.8	6.25
14.3	6.5
5.7	6.75
9.5	7
1.8	7.25
2.9	7.5

1	7.75
1	8
0.3	8.25
0.3	8.5
0.1	8.75
0.1	9

For those of you convinced that girth is what it's worth, here are the circumference figures (measuring around the penis):

Percentage of Men	Circumference (in Inches)
0.3	1.5
0.4	1.75
0.4	2
0.2	2.25
0.3	2.5
0.3	2.75
0.4	3
0.4	3.25
0.9	3.5
1.1	3.75
6.3	4
6.3	4.25
17.1	4.5
11.7	4.75
24.1	**5**
9.9	5.25

11.5	5.5
3	5.75
3.9	6
0.5	6.25
0.5	6.5
0.1	6.75

Just in case you were wondering whether this is the definitive answer to that age-old question of penis size, it's not. Another study, involving sixty men, conducted by the University of California at San Francisco, determined that the average size of their erect penises was 5.1 inches long and 4.9 inches around. A Brazilian urologist who measured 150 men reported that the average size of their erections was 5.7 inches long and 4.7 inches around.

Average weight of a Chinese man's testicles, in grams: nineteen.

Average weight of a Dane's: forty-two.

Average length of an erect penis, according to American men, in inches: ten.

Average length, according to women: four.

The longest erect penis confirmed by reliable medical data: thirteen and a half inches.

* * *

The flaccid penis averages four inches in length.

Fourteen percent of males said that they didn't enjoy sex the first time they attempted it.

Forty-one percent of women say they enjoyed sex their first time.

In an average man's semen, approximately 10 percent of his sperm is abnormal.

Women who've spent a night in jail are almost 50 percent more likely to have had more than ten lovers in the past year than women with no criminal record.

Black women are 50 percent more likely than white women to have an orgasm when they have sex.

In 1990 more than six thousand people reported injuries related to feminine hygiene products. Apparently, those instructions and diagrams provided in each box just aren't enough for some people.

Men who are castrated live an average of thirteen years longer than their uncut counterparts.

Freud may have had something there with that cigar theory,

as 70 percent of women who smoke have had more than four lovers in the last year, while 60 percent of nonsmokers had none.

Women who respond to sex surveys in magazines have had five times as many lovers as nonrespondents (and still managed to find time to fill out the survey).

Just say, "Why not?" . . . One in six adults has admitted that they agreed to have sex because they were simply too embarrassed to say no.

Some things never change . . . The average weight of a *Playboy* playmate has increased about a pound since the 1960s, to 115, and her average height increased about two inches, to five-foot-six. Her average bust size has dropped about an inch, waist size has increased an inch, and hip size has remained about the same (36-23-35).

Barbie's measurements if she were life size: 39-23-33.

Apparently, income can almost be said to be directly relational to infidelity—or, perhaps, honesty. Among those who earned less than $5,000 a year, only 16 percent of husbands admitted to cheating on their wives, while among those who made over $60,000, 70 percent had reportedly committed adultery.

* * *

In case you're counting, there are five calories in a teaspoon of semen.

And for those who like to exercise along with dieting, the average love session burns about a hundred calories.

Seven percent of American women sleep in the nude.

Twenty-five percent of teenage males feel that it's okay to be sexually active with more than one partner at a time.

Between 5 and 13 percent of physicians and mental health professionals have had some sort of sexual contact with their patients.

Thirty percent of men suffer from premature ejaculation.

Women who read romance novels tend to have twice as many lovers over the same period as those who don't.

Thirty percent of women over the age of eighty still have sexual intercourse with either their spouse or their boyfriend.

Unfortunately, one in three men over the age of sixty will suffer from impotence.

Believe it or not, the most common form of marriage is polygamy (one husband with two or more wives). One source claims that of 849 societies, 70 percent are polygamous. Polygamy may not be as widely practiced today as it once was, simply because of the prohibitive cost of keeping more than one wife.

Conversely, the least prevalent form of marriage is polyandry, which is one wife with two or more husbands. Only four of 849 societies are polyandrous.

In 1974, before AIDS became the scare it is today, the Bell survey of male homosexual promiscuity found that the average number of sexual partners in the lifetime of a gay man was one thousand.

Thirty-four percent of men and 10 percent of women have told lies in order to have sex.

According to doctors with better eyesight and more time than we have, the average ejaculate contains as many as 787 million sperm.

A male's genitals get as big as they're going to get at 14.9 years of age, on average, though late bloomers will mostly have caught up by the time they're seventeen.

At orgasm, the heart averages 140 beats per minute for men and women.

* * *

Twenty percent of heterosexual couples do not kiss every time they have sex.

According to *Cosmopolitan,* more than half of all cheating wives have affairs with married men.

When a single woman has an affair with a married man, there's a 70 percent chance that it'll be the married man who ends it.

Thirty percent of women are unable to have an orgasm on a consistent basis by any means.

About 1 percent of the adult female population are able to achieve orgasm solely through breast stimulation.

Twenty-two percent of women tell five or more friends about their first sexual experience within the week.

A recent survey found that exchanging wedding vows knocks a whole nine minutes off the average time spent making love. Married couples get it over and done with in sixteen minutes flat, while cohabiting couples spend twenty-five minutes on average in the act.

Television viewers are exposed to some form of sexual representation about twelve times per hour, or about once every five minutes.

* * *

Only one in four transvestites considers themselves gay.

Males under the age of forty are typically able to achieve an erection in less than ten seconds.

In case you're wondering, a man is considered infertile if he ejaculates fewer than 60 million sperm, of which only 40 percent or less have any motility.

During her reproductive years, the average woman will have intercourse over three thousand times.

One study found that people who work at least sixty hours a week report having more sex than those with more leisure time, averaging over five sex acts a week.

Forty percent of women report sex dreams that result in orgasm.

Typically, sperm survive only forty-eight hours within the female body; but they have been known to live as long as eight days.

Forty-three percent of women have had heterosexual anal sex.

As if they didn't have enough going for them, rich men also

statistically have the easiest time picking up women.

But if you really loved me . . . Only 4 percent of adult females have sex in order to keep a boyfriend's interest. However, 45 percent of teenage females had sex because they were pressured to.

Locker room talk aside, apparently only three out of a thousand men are well endowed enough (or at least flexible enough) to fellate themselves to orgasm.

Men consider penis size the third-most-important feature for a man, while women rated it only ninth.

Fellatio ranks as the number one sexual act desired by heterosexual men. Next, I'll tell you something you *don't* know.

Where the boys are . . . During construction of the Alaskan pipeline in the mid-1970s, prostitution arrests rose 4,000 percent.

Twelve percent of U.S. teens had their first sexual intercourse in a car.

According to a survey in *Cosmopolitan,* a woman's least favorite spot for sex is in a car.

Yes, it does happen: In 1990, 290 women were arrested in the

United States and charged with rape.

The initial spurt of ejaculate travels at twenty-eight miles per hour. In contrast, the world record for the one-hundred-yard dash is 27.1 miles per hour.

Despite the speedy head start, it still takes a sperm one hour to swim seven inches.

An unobstructed penis is capable of shooting semen anywhere from twelve to twenty-four inches.

One more thing to worry about: 80 percent of people who have a sexually transmitted disease experience no noticeable symptoms.

Four out of every five *Playboy* readers think that they're good lovers.

Only 28 percent of married men realize when their wives have cheated on them.

While men may like to brag to their friends, 47 percent of men and 42 percent of women say that they understate the number of their previous partners in order to convince someone to have sex.

Some people can't pass up a sale . . . Napoleon's withered

penis was purchased at a 1969 auction for $38,000.

Many people fancy themselves to be somewhat of a "sex-pert," but according to a 1989 Kinsey Institute study, it's far from true. Of the 1,974 individuals who participated in the test of basic sexual knowledge, only five people were able to answer correctly 95 percent of the eighteen questions asked. Over half of the test takers (55 percent) answered incorrectly 50 percent or more of the questions.

At last count, the *Playboy* archive contained just under 9 million photographs.

Thirty-nine percent of high school males think that it's okay to demand sex from a girl if they've spent a lot of money on her.

About 50 percent of U.S. workers say they've had sex in the workplace, the location of preference being the boss's desk.

A British medical journal reported a ten-year study showing that men ages forty-five to fifty-nine who had sex less often than once a month had twice the death rate of those who had sex twice a week.

Eighty percent of men surveyed reported having an orgasm during their sex dreams.

Women who live in big cities are more likely to have an affair than those who live in smaller towns.

You think you've got problems? The smallest erect penis on record was one centimeter long.

The odds of a young single woman having sex on any given night are ten to one.

Fifty percent of men who see a doctor about penile augmentation already have what's considered to be an average-sized penis.

Sperm is kept four degrees cooler than the rest of the male body.

Fifty-three percent of women prefer sex with the man on top.

Only 26 percent of women enjoy sex more than money.

Fifty-eight percent of women who've read *Playboy* think that men should be dominant.

It is reported by the world of medicine that one thirty-year-old woman had natural breasts that weighed in at fifty-two pounds.

It's estimated that over 1 million condoms are sold in the United States daily, with nearly half of them being purchased by *women.*

According to statistics, approximately 50 percent of women have one breast that's significantly larger than the other.

Eight percent of young adult males have male erectile dysfunction, or difficulty in achieving an erection.

According to a survey by *Playgirl* magazine, three out of four wives say it's more important for them to take care of their husbands than the other way around.

Only 25 percent of men planned their first sexual encounter.

Seventeen percent of women plan their first sexual encounter.

Odds are that an adolescent boy will more likely have sexual fantasies about whatever girl he's sitting next to than about a cheerleader or a movie star.

Masters and Johnson say that a woman (based on the women they've watched) can have as many as twenty orgasms an hour with the help of a vibrator.

Kind of makes you wonder what was going on . . . In 1989,

371,000 people reported injuries related to a bed, mattress, pillow, or bed linen.

The most recorded orgasms in an hour by researchers at the Center for Marital and Sexual Studies in Long Beach, California, was 134 by one female and sixteen for a male.

Our friends Masters and Johnson also published a chart documenting a woman who experienced a forty-three-second-long orgasm, consisting of at least twenty-five successive contractions.

According to *Seventeen* magazine, three out of ten boys want to marry a virgin.

According to a report from the National Opinion Research Center at the University of Chicago, high school graduates average fifty-eight sex acts a year, while those with some college average sixty-two. Those with four-year college degrees average fifty-six, and those who have been to graduate school average a paltry fifty.

Seventy-two percent of males over the age of eighty masturbate.

It takes approximately seventy days to create one sperm.

Some Americans are definitely sexier than others. About 15

percent of adults engage in half of all sexual activity.

Only 25 percent of daughters think that their mothers engage in oral sex.

Thirteen percent of females refrain from oral sex because they think that their parents would disapprove.

Considering that the typical lovemaking session averages fifteen minutes, the average couple can expect to spend 610 hours of their married lives having sex.

For every female masochist, there are twenty male masochists.

Don't ask for details, but the U.S. Center for Health Statistics reports that 2 percent of silicone breast implants are actually performed on men.

At age seventy, 73 percent of men are still potent.

According to research conducted in 1985, 20 percent of American women had a bust measurement greater than thirty-seven inches, while a similar survey in 1970 revealed that 20 percent had a measurement of less than thirty-two inches.

A woman is born with about four hundred thousand ova—

which, unlike a man's sperm, are never replenished.

A 1988–89 survey of fifteen hundred households, conducted by Tom Smith of the University of Chicago, revealed that American adults have sex an average of fifty-seven times a year, or about once a week. Another current poll of three thousand U.S. adults claimed the average was two to three times per week.

Though most will deny it, it's estimated that more than 85 percent of American females have masturbated at some time in their lives.

According to a report done in 1988 by the National Center for Health, approximately 70 percent of married American women have had premarital intercourse, and by age twenty-five, 95 percent of American females have had sex.

Only 8 percent of *Cosmopolitan* readers make love on a daily basis.

Only 12 percent of wives are more likely to initiate sex than their husbands.

On average, men aged forty-eight to sixty-five take five times longer to get an erection than those aged nineteen to thirty.

If all the sperm in an average adult testicle were laid out end to end, they'd measure a quarter mile.

One out of every two hundred women is endowed with an extra nipple.

In 1995 a Hong Kong Chi Kung master named Mo Ka Wang lifted over 250 pounds of weight two feet off the floor with only his erect penis.

Sixty-eight percent of men and 59 percent of women have been sexually involved with more than one person in their past that their current partner doesn't know about.

A twenty-five-year study by A. W. Richards, a Maryland psychotherapist and former priest, found that nearly 50 percent of Catholic priests break their vows of celibacy.

The average bra is designed to last for only 180 days of use.

According to a garment industry study, 75 percent of women wear the wrong size bra.

Sixty-six percent of pet owners surveyed claimed that they allowed their pets to remain in the bedroom during love-making.

Playgirl magazine once reported a poll in which 96 percent of wives said they had had sex at one time or another when they didn't want to.

Only 10 percent of men first learned about sex by that famous birds-and-the-bees lecture from their fathers.

Married couples still found the energy to make love 135 times a year, on average. Only 23 percent said they would like to have more sex, while 39 percent of those cohabiting complained they were still not getting enough.

Over 97 percent of breast augmentation surgery is performed on Caucasian females.

A typical orgasm lasts from three to ten seconds, with contractions occurring every 0.8 seconds for both men and women.

A 1986 Gallup poll revealed that people felt that the most "sinful" or "immoral" activities were

1. lying about a sexual disease
2. murder
3. rape
4. sexual abuse of children

Masturbation was at number 62 on the list.

A survey by DUREX condom makers found married couples had sex, on average, forty fewer times per year than couples who lived together.

There has been a dramatic increase in the percentage of female infidelity since the 1940s, when 26 percent of married women were unfaithful. In the last three decades the number has hovered around 40 percent from survey to survey.

According to one survey, 2 percent of women enjoy using feathers for sexual stimulation, and 9 percent masturbate while their partner watches.

According to most surveys, 97 percent of men masturbate, and in some circles it's felt that the remaining 3 percent are lying.

There are only about thirty-five legal brothels in Nevada.

The average woman's extramarital affair usually lasts twenty-one months.

The 37 percent of women who recently claimed that they "always enjoy sex" were typically childless, college educated, and earned over $25,000 a year.

The world record for the most illegal polygamous marriages is held by Giovanni Vigliotto of Syracuse, Sicily, who was arrested on December 30, 1981, in Panama City, Florida. He was later convicted of 104 fraudulent marriages in more than twenty-seven states and fourteen countries, spanning a period of forty-one years. Unbelievably, he married four of his victims while aboard a single cruise ship in 1968.

The largest recorded bust size for a Miss America is thirty-seven inches.

The average time a female prostitute spends in that profession is five years.

Over two hundred Americans have sex-change surgery annually.

The average age breasts begin to develop in a female is eleven.

According to Kinsey, half of the men raised on farms have had a sexual encounter with an animal.

The two leading causes of temporary impotence are prolonged cigarette smoking and tight pants.

The average single man will have had ten sex partners before tying the knot. But for women the statistic's slightly different. Fifty percent will have had fewer than four before accepting a proposal.

According to Kinsey, 75 percent of men ejaculate within three minutes of penetration.

* * *

Playboy says it takes a woman, on average, eleven minutes to reach orgasm after initial genital arousal.

Over the course of his lifetime, the average man will ejaculate approximately eighteen quarts of semen, containing about half a trillion sperm.

A telephone company receives up to nineteen cents for one minute of dial-a-porn service. While phone sex was at its peak, in 1985, Pacific Bell estimated that it earned $12 million from such 900 numbers.

The things done in the name of science . . . The research done by Masters and Johnson has involved observations of over ten thousand episodes of sexual activity.

According to the National Institute of Child Health and Human Development, the average age at which boys first engage in intercourse is 15.7 years.

When a man is sexually aroused, his testes increase in size by 50 percent.

Kinsey estimates that 30 percent of all U.S. males have experienced some kind of homosexual encounter.

Fifty-five percent of homosexual women have heterosexual

dreams.

Only 48 percent of husbands say that their wives are skilled lovers.

Only 10 percent of *Cosmo* readers said they had an orgasm the first time they had sex.

For a typical lovemaking session, the man will thrust an average of sixty to 120 times.

Currently there are estimated to be over a million full-time prostitutes in America.

Approximately 10 percent of sexually active adult women have never had an orgasm.

Sixty-six percent of runners claim they have thought about sex while running.

Eight percent said they have thought about running while engaged in sex.

A typical male will experience an average of four to five erections a night during the REM stage of sleep. Apparently, though, there's no correlation between his current sexual activity and the number of erections he does or doesn't have.

* * *

According to Kinsey and his vast amount of research, the smallest penis he came across was one and a half inches long (yes, those were erect penises).

If you're a male over thirty-five, you face a one-in-seventy-seven chance of suffering a serious heart attack during sex.

White teenage girls who live with a single mother are 60 percent more likely to have sex before the age of eighteen than those who live with both parents, though the percentage is much lower for black girls.

Women who lost their virginity before their eighteenth birthday are twice as likely to be sexually active in adulthood than those who waited.

Twenty percent of women who live with their boyfriends have another sex partner.

One in three men cheats on his partner, while only one in four women cheats.

One in four women can't remember the name of all their past lovers.

Seventy percent of both men and women admit that they have fantasized about someone else while having sex.

Nearly 25 percent of psychologists, psychiatrists, social workers, and other mental health professionals have had sexual contact with their patients, many citing "client welfare" as the reason.

Almost two-thirds of women have faked an orgasm at one time or another.

Currently, the average age at which women begin menstruating is 12.8 years. That age has continued to decrease by four months every decade since 1830.

Latino women of childbearing years are statistically more sexually active than either black or white women of the same age bracket.

3 When Sex Goes Horribly Awry

It takes all kinds. Just as there are those who suffer coronaries if you don't put the cap back on the toothpaste tube, there are those whose enjoyment of sex is entirely contingent on something most people wouldn't dream about. While most of us are content to enjoy what many would call "typical" hetero- and homosexual encounters, it is irrefutable that some decidedly different folks prefer some seriously different strokes.

And as with anything enjoyable in life, things can become wretchedly unpleasant when sex begins to go awry.

Sexual Hang-Ups

Some people's idea of being sexually adventurous is making love in the hallway instead of the bedroom, while others aren't content unless they're able to caress their lover's eyeballs with their tongue. If you are interested in the truly unusual sexual fetishes of others, the following section is for you.

Acrotomophilia: A sexual attraction to amputees. Some psychologists hypothesize that acrotomophiliac men suffer from castration anxiety, thus viewing a female amputee as a castrated male, and perhaps harboring some sadistic impulses toward women.

Agalmatophilia: This is the fetish for statues or mannequins. Some people have an uncontrollable desire to masturbate whenever they see a nude mannequin.

Apotemnophilia: Describes people who are aroused by the idea of losing a limb, surgically or otherwise. While this fetish is usually limited to fantasy, some apotemnophiliacs have injured themselves to such an extent as to require amputation by a surgeon.

Autophagy: The practice of eating your own flesh for sexual kicks. One man who became obsessed with the urge to bite off and eat women's skin carried a pair of scissors for years in the hope of carrying out such a deed. While never successful, after certain close encounters he would instead cut off and eat a piece of his own skin, which would result in immediate orgasm.

Dendrophilia: People with this condition prefer trees to humans as sex partners, with some men using holes in the bark as vaginal substitutes. It's believed by some psychiatrists that these men fear their own homosexual impulses and deal with the fear by finding a vagina in a phallic object. Brings a whole new meaning to the word "woodpecker."

Emetophilia: A fetish for throwing up and being thrown up on—an action also known as a Roman shower (if anyone knew how to have a good time, it was the Romans). Some shrinks have said that this preference may hark back to infancy, when throwing up often led to receiving a lot of love and attention.

Formicophilia: This is a fetish for having small insects crawl on your genitals. Some may consider humans too threatening as a sex partner, so formicophiliacs look for a more controllable sexual outlet. Insects never reject you, plus you can always kill them if things get too difficult.

Oculolinctus: An apparently rare fetish wherein people are sexually aroused by licking a partner's eyeball. In fact, there's one reported case of a female who was unable to have an orgasm unless she licked the eyeball of her obliging lover. A word of caution before you try this at home: oral herpes can be transferred to the eye.

Taphephilia: The tendency to get turned on by the idea of being buried alive. While this may seem too odd to comprehend, some psychiatrists have speculated that burial suggests a warm, safe, earthen womb for the person who may have been deprived of parental affection in childhood.

Zoophilia: Obviously, a desire for sex with animals. It's felt that zoophiliac men prefer the "no strings attached" relationship of a sheep to that of an emotional woman.

Sexual Medical Meltdowns

Like everything else in life, sex comes with its own set of disasters. While most people never face anything more frustrating than occasional impotence, following are some of the things that can *really* go wrong sexually.

Dominican Republic syndrome: A rare disorder, first discovered in the Dominican Republic, whereby persons are born anatomically female but, at the onset of puberty, develop male genitalia and other masculine characteristics. If you're concerned, don't fret it. Since this hereditary condition was first discovered, in the mid-1970s, there have been only thirty-eight documented cases, all in the Dominican Republic. The Spanish term for this condition is *guevodoces,* which means "penis at twelve."

Elephantiasis: Sufferers of this condition can have their testicles swell to the size of their heads. This is caused by the obstruction of the lymphatic channels in the affected area, causing fluid to build up. In tropical countries, the most common cause is infestation by species of small roundworms in the lymphatic system. One such sufferer had a testicle weigh in excess of 150 pounds and had to use a wheelbarrow to get around. Thankfully, modern medicine has a quick and painless cure that simply kills the roundworm.

Micropenis: A fortunately rare disorder where the afflicted suffers from an unusually small penis, roughly three-quarters to one inch long (yes, that is erect).

Penile-enhancement blunders: Dr. Melvyn Rosenstein, who claims to be "the world's leading authority on penile surgery," had his license temporarily suspended by the Medical Board of California. More than forty of his former patients claim that he botched their surgeries so badly that they suffer from symptoms such as intense pain, scarring, deformities, loss of feeling, and in some cases a *decrease* in size. The doctor has testified the complaints resulted from professional jealousy and disgruntled employees.

But that's nothing compared to a 1993 report in the *Bangkok Post* about quacks operating in Thailand who performed at least a hundred bogus penis-enlargement operations. The surgery involved injections of a mixture of olive oil and chalk, among various other substances. One hospital official noted that he had even seen victims' penises containing portions of the Bangkok telephone directory.

Just keep in mind that among the risks of penile implants are infection, which can lead to gangrene and amputation, as well as migration of the implant device to another part of the body.

Peyronie's disease: This is caused by a buildup of fibrous plaque in the penis, specifically in the fibroelastic walls of the blood chambers of the penis. This plaque buildup causes the penis to develop a curve, or bend, in it. In some cases, this can be very painful.

Priapism: This involves a prolonged and painful erection, brought on by disease, that can last from several hours to a few days. The initial thrill of staying erect throughout the night gives way to fear once the penis begins to hurt, which naturally begins to make life a bit more difficult. The treatment involves making small incisions along the base of the penis to bleed it. Priapism is named after the ancient Greek god of procreation, the permanently erect Priapus.

Steatopygia: A medical condition resulting in an extreme accumulation of fat on the buttocks. This is not merely being a bit overweight. Women suffering from this generally have buttocks that each measure two to three feet across. Another frightening aspect of this is sometimes long labia minora that hang down between the knees.

Torsion of the testicles: A condition whereby the glands in your scrotum become tangled in such a web of knots you feel like you've just been kicked in the nuts by an entire football team.

Sexual Phobias

Phobias aren't just a slight aversion to something, but a crippling fear that seriously affects a person's way of life. Most people, for example, have a general fear of heights, but those with acrophobia can't even consider scaling a tall structure without breaking out in a sweat and breathing heavily. With that in mind, consider these sexual phobias:

coitophobia: fear of coitus
cypridophobia: fear of prostitutes or venereal disease
defecaloesiophobia: fear of painful bowel movements
dishabiliophobia: fear of undressing in front of someone
erotophobia: fear of sexual love or sexual questions
eurotophobia: fear of female genitalia
gymnophobia: fear of nudity

hedonophobia: fear of feeling pleasure

heterophobia: fear of the opposite sex

homophobia: fear of homosexuality or of becoming homosexual

ithyphallophobia: fear of seeing, thinking about, or having an erect penis

kolpophobia: fear of genitals, particularly female

luiphobia: fear of lues, or syphilis

malaxophobia: fear of love play

medomalacuphobia: fear of losing an erection

medorthophobia: fear of an erect penis

menophobia: fear of menstruation

oneirogmophobia: fear of wet dreams

paraphobia: fear of sexual perversion

parthenophobia: fear of virgins or young girls

phallophobia: fear of a penis, especially erect

rectophobia: fear of the rectum or rectal diseases

rhypophobia: fear of defecation

scatophobia: fear of fecal matter

syphilophobia: fear of syphilis

venustraphobia: fear of beautiful women

4 Animal Lust

While sex among humans ranges from the moderately intriguing to the wildly bizarre, nothing compares to the even stranger goings-on in the animal kingdom. Sure, there are those few who can think of nothing more sexually exciting than to lick another's eyeballs (oculolinctus), but that doesn't compare with females who eat their lovers before, during, and after copulation (praying mantises) or males whose genitals literally explode at climax, killing them as they plug the female (bees). While birds do it and bees do it, it's the way they do it that makes for some fascinating reading.

The largest living animal, the blue whale, naturally

enough also has the largest penis, measuring approximately ten feet long and one foot in diameter. The penis of its cousin the sperm whale gets as big as nine feet long. And yes, the sperm whale is so named because early sailors thought those gallons of white, gooey oil found in its head was indeed sperm.

The Alpine banana slug is only six inches long but has a penis measuring over thirty-two inches.

The fruit fly *Drosophila bifurca* has sperm six centimeters long, or twenty times longer than its entire body length.

Mosquitoes perform a sex act that lasts only two seconds.

The ten-inch banana slugs of the Northwest end their thirty-hour hermaphroditic mating session by chewing off each other's male sex organs.

Long a symbol of sexual potency, the rhinoceros can ejaculate ten times or more during his half-hour session with a female. He also has a penis that is two feet long.

Though barnacles can't move, they still mate via an extraordinarily long penis (150 percent of their body length) that reaches over and into the female's mantle cavity.

The northern right whale has a pair of gonads that weighs as much as twenty-two hundred pounds. Such massive testicles are a product of evolution known as "sperm competition." Whenever a female goes into heat, she's accosted by dozens of randy male whales eager to have their sperm be the one. Each successive male hopes to have his untold gallons of sperm wash out his competition's.

Capuchin monkeys usually say hello by showing one another their erections.

Female chimpanzees have been observed masturbating with their fingers, twigs, and a water faucet.

Cows are sometimes made to wear a type of brassiere to keep them from stepping on their udders (ouch!).

A drone honeybee will wait his whole life for one chance to mate with a queen. As soon as the queen opens her sting chamber to receive him, he explodes, his genitals bursting like a detonating grenade. Plugged, the queen flies away, leaving the drone to fall to the ground dead and eviscerated, albeit with a smile on his face.

The praying mantis is even stranger. Upon commencement of conjugal activities, the female mantis will proceed to bite off the head of the male. In typical male fashion, however, he doesn't let missing something as insignificant as a head keep him from completing his task. He's able to impregnate the female, as well as provide her with postcoital munchies as she finishes what she started. It's often been reported that sometimes the female will bite off the male's head even before they've begun mating. Again, this fails to slow him down, and despite being headless, he manages to grope his way to fatherhood.

The female green bonellia is a meter-long marine animal that is quite literally a thousand times larger than her male counterpart. The prospective mate will slide its millimeter-long body down the female's enormous trunk, through her mouth and into her gullet, and then bore through into her genital tract, where he fertilizes her eggs.

If you urinate when swimming in a South American river, you may encounter the candiru. Drawn to warmth, this tiny fish is known to follow a stream of urine to its source, swim inside the body, and flare its barbed fins. There it will remain firmly embedded until surgically removed.

Fleas are known to engage in sex immediately after feasting on rabbit's blood, specifically, if the opportunity presents itself.

Human birth control pills also work on gorillas (though gorillas reportedly keep forgetting to take them, too).

A male African antelope will continue to mate until he drops from exhaustion.

The male gypsy moth can smell the virgin female gypsy moth from 1.8 miles away.

An elephant can be pregnant for up to two years.

A desert rat called the Shaw's jird has been witnessed copulating 224 times in two hours with the same mate.

Animals in the wild rarely experience the joys of venereal disease (except for otters, who can get herpes).

Earthworms like to mate head-to-tail, and do so for anywhere from two to three hours at a time.

Gorilla penises are only a third the size of an average man's.

Hamsters can have sex up to seventy-five times a day, and prefer to do it face-to-face.

Humans aren't the only female animals that can experience orgasm; some rabbits and ferrets do as well.

If a male bottlenose dolphin rubs himself on the back of a passing turtle, he is more than likely masturbating.

Most insects will remain locked in embrace, as it were, for at least twenty-four hours.

Perhaps the originator of the quickie, a baboon engages in a sex session that typically lasts all of fifteen seconds (though one reportedly bragged to his baboon buddies of lasting twice as long).

Spanish fly is actually made from the wings of beetles.

The Abyssinian bat's penis is covered with stiff bristles.

The beaver mates for only three minutes but does so in the missionary style.

The long, hook-shaped bone of a raccoon's penis has been used as a toothpick.

The mole shrew has a penis shaped like the letter *S*.

The walrus has the largest penis of any land mammal, measuring twenty-four and a half inches when erect.

Most birds have no true penis, but merely vents that must be carefully aligned with the female's vent to allow sperm to enter and fertilize.

Swans are the only birds with penises.

* * *

A whale's penis is called a "dork," which, incidentally, is where we get the derogatory slang.

Some carnivores, rodents, bats, and insectivores have a penis bone, called a baculum.

Iguanas, koalas, and Komodo dragons all have penises that are split in two, allowing them more easily to have either left-handed or right-handed mating.

You think you have it bad . . . Because female gorillas are in heat only six days in a four-year cycle, most male gorillas are lucky if they get any once a year.

Some female hyenas have a pseudopenis.

Only humans and horses have hymens.

After a male dog mounts a female, he usually gets trapped in her vagina, sometimes for as long as thirty minutes.

The true lemming of Scandinavia can become pregnant at the age of fourteen days, with a gestation period of sixteen to twenty-four days.

The mottled sand grasshopper will literally jump on anything that moves in order to mate quickly before a predator strikes. This instinct has led grasshoppers to try mating with males and females alike and even with completely unrelated species.

Bee wolves are even worse. During mating season, they'll stand on conspicuous perches and fly toward almost anything that passes by. While this usually results in the prospective mate being a female bee wolf, it has been known to also result in flying straight into the jaws of a robber fly, a vicious predator of the bee wolf.

Most whale sex usually lasts only a few seconds.

Porpoises have been known to engage in group sex.

The sperm of a mouse is actually longer than the sperm of an elephant.

Some fish have been known to engage in fellatio.

Once the female bee wolf has mated, her libido takes a nose-dive. In fact, male bee wolves have been known to be stung to death by recently impregnated females who were more concerned with tending to their nest than with a good time.

One ejaculation from a bull could theoretically inseminate three hundred cows.

After what is sometimes hours of orchestrated flight by a

multitude of male mayflies, the female object of affection will make an appearance, only to be immediately grabbed by several males at once, with as many as four holding on to her and one another until she lands and one male succeeds in mating with her.

Crabs like to copulate face-to-face.

One of the reasons male deer rub their antlers on a tree or the ground is to masturbate.

Pigs do indeed have a corkscrew-shaped penis. When engaged in sex, the male's penis will make semirotary actions until it becomes firmly secured in the folds of the female's cervix, at which point the male ejaculates, a process that in itself takes as long as thirty minutes.

Female baboons have been known to engage in a primitive form of prostitution by stealing food during sex.

The average mink sexual encounter lasts for several hours (how do you think they get their coats so shiny?).

The current record for the longest rattlesnake mating session is 22.75 hours.

When a female rhinoceros is feeling in the mood, she'll ram her potential lover with her horn (haven't you ever heard of the term "horny"?).

The female bedbug is born without any external sex organs, so the male bedbug has to use his pointed penis to drill a hole into his partner's gut and deposit his sperm into her bloodstream. During long spells without access to human blood, the female's been known to dine on her male partner's semen.

5 The Unkindest Cut of All

Ritual mutilation of the digit of one's manhood hasn't been limited to circumcision, which dates back to nearly the beginning of recorded history. While most men cringe at the mere mention of John Wayne Bobbit, castration and similar modifications of the most sacred of male organs haven't always been a punishment. In fact, there was a time when castration was encouraged by clergy or parents, and even favored by the potential castrati themselves, though the market for castrati isn't what it once was. Following are some of the more leg-crossing, teeth-clenching historical facts regarding that unkindest cut of all.

America's most common surgical procedure is circumcision.

During the Victorian era, it was believed that epilepsy was due to being in a state of constant sexual arousal, seizures being a sexual release of sorts—which naturally led to the belief that, for male epileptics, castration would provide the cure.

It wasn't until the twentieth century that New Jersey and Wisconsin threw out laws allowing castration of epileptics.

Impresarios used to have choirboys castrated so that they could continue to sing soprano as adults in the best cathedrals in Europe. The last male soprano, Alessandro Moreschi, died in 1922, leaving behind a gramophone recording of a voice that was as high and flexible as a woman's but as robust and powerful as a man's.

Full testicular and penile castration required that the castratee be strapped by his arms and legs to a table. A cord was then tied around his genitals, which were quickly amputated with a sharp razor. A red-hot poker or molten tar would then be used to cauterize the wound. If you survived the loss of blood—eight in ten did not—you were given a liquid diet until you built up enough bladder pressure to force a stream of urine through the soft scar tissue.

In ancient China, a man who'd been convicted of killing his

father would be punished by being castrated.

In some Native American tribes, defeated foes were castrated by women of the conquering tribe, who removed their manhood in more ways than one. Though you might think that this custom was developed to serve as one final emotional blow to the enemy's gender ego, this wasn't the case. The task of castrating the fallen was simply considered too menial and therefore left to the squaws, while the long, drawn-out torture was reserved for the braves.

Fifth-century Samaritans would take a convicted rapist or adulterer and tie him upside down by his genitals. They would then tie one hand behind his back and put a sharp knife in the other. If he chose to free himself, he would have to perform self-castration.

Throughout the centuries, eunuchs were heavily in demand so that one could have a docile, sexually harmless male to oversee one's harem. In Roman society eunuchs were considered too docile to pose any threat to the ever-wary emperors, and were considered "safe" to be cooks and bedchamber servants, as well as "wives" to the hedonistic Roman emperors.

Talk about not wanting to work . . . During times when the Chinese government sought to curtail population growth, some Chinese were known to remove their own testes to obtain both the pension and the dispensation from labor that the government offered willing males.

Castrati had only their testicles removed, not the penis. While the loss of testosterone made castrati facially hairless, gave them rounded butts and hips, and allowed them to have smooth skin, many were still able to get an erection, keep it, and use it, though they had semenless orgasms.

Genitals were considered war trophies, with penises being prized over testicles. One victory of the Egyptians over their Libyan enemies resulted in 13,230 penises.

Many an ancient monument and stone relief sports conquerors brandishing the genitalia of their fallen enemies. One such relief, found in Thebes, displays the mustering of victims' genitalia in a recent conquest, with the inscription *Prisoners brought before the king, 1000; phalli, 3000.*

King Henry II of England became so incensed at the refusal of many of the local priests to side with him that he ordered them to be castrated and the trophies brought to him on a platter.

In fifth-century B.C. Greece, many underwent testicular castration under the misconception that it would prevent hernia, epilepsy, and mental illness, since eunuchs never seemed to suffer from these ailments.

* * *

During the fifth century, testicular castration was believed to be a last-ditch effort to cure the plague as well as elephantiasis.

Roman Catholic clergy were usually at the forefront in promoting adolescent castration between the seventeenth and nineteenth centuries: One French diocese is reported to have castrated five hundred boys—though the operation involved only one testicle, as it was felt that removing both was a bit excessive.

Pierre Dronis wrote of one French female castratrix whose clients were so numerous that the castrated gonads served as her dog's sole source of food.

The French Royal Society of Medicine put an end to the practice of castration, not on the basis of its disappointing results but because it created so few men fit for military service. The practice was continued on the mentally ill in the hope of curing their derangements, though it never did.

In ancient, pre-Christian Rome, the primary use for eunuchs—labeled *voluptas* for their feminine shape—was for the sexual pleasure of the wealthy. Men and women alike could enjoy the sexual pleasure of a eunuch without fear of offspring.

* * *

In ancient Rome, public sentiment stated that eunuchs, not the nobility who took advantage of them, were responsible for moral decline.

Around 200 A.D., castrati were so common that one could be bought for a single talent, a small silver coin.

Because the most important prerequisite for civil service in the third century was castration, parents willingly mutilated their sons in order to help their advancement.

Pope Clement VIII was so impressed when he heard castrati sing in 1599 that he sanctioned emasculated men as singers, and within twenty-five years all adult singers in the Vatican choir were castrati.

The first "star" castrato, Ferri, died at age seventy, worth $3 million in today's money. It was exactly because of the promise of such wealth that so much masculinity was lost, though only a handful of castrati ever saw similar success.

One of the undesirable side effects of being castrated after puberty is obesity.

The original purpose of circumcision in the Western world for non-Jewish males was to curb masturbation, as it was the presence of a tight, gripping foreskin, many felt, that caused such perpetual arousal.

* * *

Because of constant ridicule at fifth-century Greek gymnasia from their uncircumcised Greek friends, many Jews sought reconstructive foreskin surgery, which pulled the remaining skin over the glans penis and tied it until it was completely stretched out.

During Elizabethan times, one physician encouraged circumcision to curtail masturbation because "the effects range from impotence to epilepsy, and include consumption, blindness, imbecility, insanity, rheumatism, gonorrhea, priapism, tumors, constipation, hemorrhoids, female homosexuality, and finally the shameful habit leads to death."

The Puritans had such an obsessive fear of masturbation that almost any means were employed to curtail the practice. One commentator wrote that "some doctors recommend covering the penis with plaster of Paris, or leather, or making the lad wear a chastity belt or spiked rings."

A standard American medical textbook of the early 1900s claimed that the foreskin leads to "nocturnal incontinence, hysteria, epilepsy, and feeble-mindedness."

American pediatricians in the 1940s needed only to turn to their copy of the standard *Diseases of Infancy and Childhood* to see that learned people "advocate female circumcision, cauterization of the clitoris, and even blistering of the vulva and prepuce for recalcitrant female masturbators."

In Arab countries, it used to be a common practice to have prostitutes tightened by surgical mutilation, to increase their value on the market as "fresh women."

6 They Said What?!

Considering how well scrutinized every action, word, and deed of the rich and famous has become, it's a wonder they've gotten away with saying some of the things they have. Here is a list of what many have (reportedly) said in interviews, to friends, and to themselves.

"You're only as old as the women you feel."

—Groucho Marx

"Because sheep can't type."

—Former senator Armbrister of Texas, when asked why God invented women

"My big fantasy has been to seduce a priest."

—Linda Ronstadt

"I gave up rock 'n' roll for the rock of ages. I used to be a glaring homosexual until God changed me."

—Little Richard

"I have committed adultery in my heart many times."

—Jimmy Carter

"His lust is in his heart? I hope it's a little lower."

—Shirley MacLaine, referring to Jimmy Carter

"I think he's a joke, with all that fag dancing."

—John Lennon, talking about Mick Jagger

"I'd rather be watching you in bed with my wife."

—Presidential candidate Barry Goldwater, when asked if he'd appear on a talk show

"I should think so. I've had enough practice."

—Rod Stewart, after being asked if he was a good lover

"I've been sucked by the biggest names in Hollywood."

—James Dean

"I was too polite to ask."

—Gore Vidal, on whether his first sexual

experience was with a man or a woman

"Three minutes of serious sex and I need eight hours of sleep and a bowl of Wheaties."

—Richard Pryor

"I've never slept with a cheerleader. I'm allergic to pom-poms."

—Bubba Smith

"I haven't had that many women; only as many as I could lay my hands on."

—Dudley Moore

"I like to hurt women when I make love to them . . . to see them bleed."

—Mike Tyson

"Only good girls keep diaries. Bad girls don't have time."

—Roseanne

"[He's a] Pelvic Missionary. He's laid more ugly women than you'd ever believe."

—Muhammad Ali's doctor

"I always knew Frank would end up in bed with a boy."

—Ava Gardner, referring to Frank Sinatra and Mia Farrow

* * *

"[They've become] sloppy eaters and sloppy lovers."

—Barbara Cartland, on the English

"We are powerless in cases of oral-genital intimacy, unless it obstructs interstate commerce."

—J. Edgar Hoover

"I need sex like I need food."

—Barbra Streisand

"Anything that can't be done in bed isn't worth doing."

—Groucho Marx

"Here's how to relieve an upsex stomach . . . I mean, with sex lax . . . Ex-Lax."

—Johnny Carson blooper

"His head looks like my crotch."

—Roseanne, on Don King

"The first time I masturbated, it flew across the room."

—Jack Lemmon

"If God had meant to have homosexuals, he would have created Adam and Bruce."

—Anita Bryant

"Bisexuality immediately doubles your chances for a date on Saturday night."

—Woody Allen

"Older guys like to receive head but they don't like to give it."

—Victoria Principal

"Very few people suck toes. They think it's foot fetishism."

—Barbra Streisand

"[The bedroom is] not a place for screwing. It is a form of paradise."

—Rod Steiger

"I do all my best work in bed."

—Mae West

"Young lady, yours is a case of arrested development. With your development, someone is bound to get arrested."

—Groucho Marx

"I wish I had as much in bed as I get in the newspapers."

—Linda Ronstadt

"Women who think they manipulate the world by pussy power are fools."

—Writer and feminist Germaine Greer

"Onstage, I make love to twenty-five thousand people, and then I go home alone."

—Janis Joplin

"I dress for women and undress for men."

—Angie Dickinson

"I've never been guilt-free about sex. I'm Catholic."

—Joe Piscopo

"If it hadn't been Errol Flynn, I wouldn't even have remembered it."

—Truman Capote

"There is no greater pleasure than that of bodily love."

—Plato

"She has lilacs for pubic hair."

—Blake Edwards, discussing his wife, Julie Andrews

"Do it quick, my wife would say. Get it over with as fast as you can."

—The Boston Strangler

"If I had as many love affairs as you give me credit for, I would be speaking to you from a jar at the Harvard Medical School."

—Frank Sinatra

* * *

"The way to resolve a situation with a woman is to jump on her."

—Lee Marvin

"I'm never done with a girl until I've had her three ways."

—John F. Kennedy

"Any girl who doesn't want to screw can leave right now."

—Babe Ruth

"If I had jumped on all the dames I was supposed to have jumped on, I would never have had any time to go fishing."

—Clark Gable

"The first girl you go to bed with is always pretty."

—Walter Matthau

"I'm not an authority on sex. I'm more of a fan."

—George Burns

"Women would come up and show me their breasts and ask my opinion. And I'd give it to them."

—Mark Harmon

"The books say we're supposed to have penis envy, but look who wrote the books."

—Yoko Ono

* * *

"The only unnatural sex act is one which you cannot perform."

—Alfred Kinsey

"He doesn't even take his boots off."

—Eva Braun, on her future husband, Adolf Hitler's, romantic interludes

"My favorite hobby? Oh, come on now. You know what it is."

—Stan Laurel

"He's hung like a horse."

—Clara Bow, commenting on Gary Cooper

"There are some things you can get in the mood for all the time, and sex is one of them."

—Jimmy Connors

"The older a woman gets, the more interested they are in her."

—Agatha Christie, on why she preferred archaeologists

"At one time, I was considered quite sexless."

—Katharine Hepburn

"Nothing. She just has to lie there."

—Richard Burton, on what makes a woman good in bed

* * *

"I knew her before she was a virgin."

—Oscar Levant, on Doris Day

"The first time I slept with a girl, I didn't know where to put my peter."

—Baseball manager Billy Martin

"I have steak at home. Why go out for hamburger?"

—Paul Newman, on infidelity

"The whole thing lasted about a minute and a half, and that included buying the dress."

—Joan Rivers, on her first time

"Working in Hollywood gives one a certain expertise in the field of prostitution."

—Jane Fonda

"I want the same things all men do, Rice Krispies and some sucking."

—Dudley Moore

"There's got to be more than this."

—Victoria Principal, remembering her feelings after her first sexual experience

* * *

"Poorly."

—Shere Hite's response to the question "How have most men had sex with you?"

"He could do anything with me except have normal intercourse, because that would be cheating on his wife."

—Marilyn Chambers, on Sammy Davis Jr.

"I used to look through peepholes. It messed me up sexually."

—Richard Pryor

"Not if he comes looking for it in my room."

—Bubba Smith, on being asked if a homosexual could find happiness in the NFL

"I couldn't pee without it hurting for a month."

—Loretta Lynn, on her first time

"I'll bet he doesn't put his hand up her dress."

—Marilyn Monroe, commenting on John and Jackie Kennedy

"I love men. I love sex and I don't care who knows it."

—Margot Kidder

"If I hadn't had them, I would have had some made."

—Dolly Parton

* * *

"Her breasts hung over the picture like a thunderstorm."

—A movie critic's comments on Jane Russell's appearance in *The Outlaw*

"Let's just say I've gotten laughs in bed."

—Steve Martin

"If a heterosexual woman had cut the same erotic swath, people would call her a slut."

—Martina Navratilova, on Magic Johnson

"That's what I am to the world today, a phallic symbol."

—Errol Flynn

"The reason I feel so guilty about masturbation is that I'm so bad at it."

—David Steinberg

"When a man sits with a pretty girl for an hour, it seems like a minute. That's relativity."

—Albert Einstein

"I don't think everyone conceives of sex the way I do—surrealistic and rich with humor."

—Woody Allen

* * *

"If you suck a tit, you're rated X; but if you cut it off with a sword, you're PG."

—*Jack Nicholson*

"The only alliance I would make with women's lib is in bed."

—*Abbie Hoffman*

"Will you invite me to come here again?"

—*Errol Flynn, to Hedda Hopper after he masturbated on her front door*

"When a woman comes, it's a sensual experience you cannot have when screwing a man."

—*Tennessee Williams*

"I've only slept with the men I've been married to."

—*Elizabeth Taylor, remarking on how she should be considered quite promiscuous*

"Homosexuality is a sickness, like baby rape or wanting to become the head of General Motors."

—*Eldridge Cleaver*

"Men aren't attracted to me by my mind. They're attracted to me by what I don't mind."

—*Gypsy Rose Lee*

"[I] played bump-and-grind joints where the stripper had a

damned horse in her act."

—Bob Seger, commenting on having to pay his dues

"A vacuum with nipples."

—Otto Preminger, describing Marilyn Monroe

"I'm pure as the driven slush."

—Tallulah Bankhead

"Rare are those who prefer virtue to the pleasures of sex."

—Confucius

"Honolulu smells like sex."

—Andy Warhol

"Homosexuals are crazy about me because I'm so flamboyant."

—Mae West

"I was just checking Nasty for snakebites."

—Rob Lowe, when caught in a compromising position with another woman

"When he dies, they're giving his zipper to the Smithsonian."

—Dean Martin, on Frank Sinatra

In his later years Groucho Marx said that he would trade all of his fame and fortune for an erection.

* * *

"Three, four, or five times was not unusual for him."

—*Joan Collins, on Warren Beatty*

"I don't know if I do it right."

—*Marilyn Monroe, to Marlon Brando*

Benjamin Franklin recommended sex with older women because "they are so grateful."

Brave New World author Aldous Huxley called chastity "the most unnatural of sexual perversions."

Despite having plenty of women who wanted to sleep with him, Clark Gable still went to prostitutes because "I can pay them to go away."

Director Roman Polanski fled the United States after pleading guilty to having sex with a thirteen-year-old girl. "For some reason, young girls like me," he said.

Shakespeare referred to the penis as "the dart of love" and "the potato finger," among other things.

The merry seventeenth-century English monarch Charles II said, "I do not interfere with the souls of women, only their bodies."

7 Sex Styles of the Rich and Famous

No one will be surprised to know that the rich and famous not only indulge; they also have a few of their own little sexual hang-ups and fetishes. And there are some just plain interesting facts about their sex lives.

Jane Russell had twin Alaskan mountain peaks named in her honor.

Jean Harlow used to keep ice cubes on the movie set in order to keep her nipples hard.

In 1961, Elvis Presley said he had slept with over a thousand women.

Howard Hughes's aversion to dogs came about after one bit him on the penis in 1940.

Henry Fonda once noted that if he hadn't said "yuck" to Lucille Ball the morning after, the Desilu studio might have been called Henry-Lu.

Nelson Rockefeller reportedly died while having sex with his mistress.

According to one of his mistresses, JFK's greatest asset in bed was his sense of humor.

Many claim that the cause of Sir Isaac Newton's acute insomnia was sexual frustration. He died a virgin.

Critics would determine the success of a Tom Jones concert by the number of panties thrown on the stage.

Big feet were a turnoff for Elvis Presley.

Behind the Green Door star Marilyn Chambers said that in truth, she'd actually be embarrassed to go to an orgy.

William Masters and Virginia Johnson Masters first met while studying how people reach orgasm.

Babe Ruth's roommates complained frequently about his

loud lovemaking.

At Errol Flynn's rape trial, the teenaged victim complained that "he did it with his shoes on," shortly before the release of his film *They Died with Their Boots On.*

Alice in Wonderland author Lewis Carroll had a thing for photographing prepubescent girls.

Reportedly having the largest penis in Hollywood, Milton Berle was told by a friend just before a size contest, "Only take out enough to win."

Famous French actress Sarah Bernhardt was accused of seducing all the European heads of state, including the pope.

Leonardo da Vinci was bisexual.

Rudy Vallee claimed to have had his first heterosexual encounter when he was six years old.

Rudolph Valentino married two lesbians during his lifetime.

Rudolph Valentino supposedly had trouble consummating his marriages.

Later in life, Vivian Leigh went mad and was found roaming the streets as a pickup.

* * *

Adolf Hitler was reportedly a coprophiliac (he had a thing for women's feces, as well as being urinated on by women).

Jack Lemmon says that the first time he made love he was upside down with his foot caught in the seat of his car.

John Holmes reportedly had a fourteen-inch penis, though it's never been verified by reliable medical sources.

In the 1920s, mobster Lucky Luciano controlled two hundred madams and thousands of prostitutes.

Shel Silverstein, author of the popular children's poetry book *Where the Sidewalk Ends,* was at one time a prolific *Playboy* humorist.

Clyde Barrow, of Bonnie and Clyde fame, was reportedly impotent.

Ernest Hemingway's member was once described as "the size of a 30-30 rifle shell."

Charlie Chaplin was considered to be quite well endowed.

Jean Harlow was the first actress to appear regularly in the talkies without a bra.

* * *

German composer Richard Wagner was said to have an "incurable predilection for other men's wives."

Many have felt that Wyatt Earp was a pimp because so many of his relatives were prostitutes.

Steely Dan got their name from a sexual device depicted in the book *The Naked Lunch.*

Bette Midler claims that she was drugged and groped by Geraldo.

One of Sylvester Stallone's less famous roles is in the retitled stag film *The Italian Stallion.*

Call of the Wild author Jack London was so well endowed, his friends called him "the Stallion."

In her book, *Passion and Betrayal,* Gennifer Flowers claims that she used to tie Bill Clinton to the bedpost and that she's far better at sex than his wife, Hillary.

While engaged in secretive indiscretions with Donna Rice, presidential hopeful Gary Hart was photographed aboard a boat named *Monkey Business.*

The girlfriend of W. C. Fields ended up marrying the private eye Fields sent to spy on her.

* * *

Charles Laughton liked his male lovers to be young and in need of his money because, as he once said, "I have got a face like an elephant's behind."

Pauline Bonaparte (Napoleon's sister) had chronic acute abdominal pain that was caused by excessive intercourse.

Mickey Mantle liked to peek under hotel room doors with mirrors.

Kenny Rogers was sued by three women who claimed that he forced them into playing kinky phone-sex games.

Howard Hughes reportedly spent more money on his sex life than anyone in history; but he gave sex up completely in the early sixties because of his overwhelming fear of germs.

Before he became president, General Dwight D. Eisenhower's little soldier failed to salute during his first two attempts at adultery.

The famous Notre Dame football coach Knute Rockne got the idea for his famous Four Horsemen's back shift formation while watching a chorus line in a girlie show.

Meryl Streep, in order to save her energy for the camera, abstains from sex while filming a movie.

* * *

Julius Caesar was known as the husband of every woman and the wife of every man.

Beethoven's deafness was most likely caused by syphilis.

Vincent van Gogh had a live-in sexual relationship with just one woman, and she was a prostitute. No wonder he cut off his ear.

Three Musketeers author Alexandre Dumas died of syphilis. He was also quoted as saying, "I need several mistresses. If I had only one, she'd be dead within a week."

The famous Mormon leader Brigham Young fathered fifty-six children and left behind seventeen wives (wouldn't you name a college after him too?).

Howard Hughes reportedly claimed that he created an aerodynamic bra for Jane Russell in her film *The Outlaw.*

Mel Gibson had his behind shaved for the movie *Lethal Weapon 2.*

Marie Antoinette's breasts were used to mold a drinking-goblet just prior to the French Revolution.

Horatio Alger was fired as minister of the Unitarian church

in Brewster, Massachusetts, because his hands had a tendency to wander when he ministered to little boys.

Elvira, Mistress of the Dark, began her career as a pornographic redhead.

Like mother like daughter . . . Both Judy Garland and her daughter Liza Minnelli had homosexual husbands.

Noted English art critic John Ruskin refused to consummate his marriage once he discovered that his bride had pubic hair.

Cleopatra was rumored to have fellated over one hundred noblemen in one evening.

At the time of his death, Napoleon was so riddled with disease his penis had shrunk to only one inch.

Napoleon preferred to have sex with Josephine when she was unwashed, remarking, too, that she had the prettiest rear end he'd ever seen.

Martin Luther King Jr. thought that virginity was sexually undesirable.

Johann Sebastian Bach fathered twenty children during his lifetime.

* * *

Famous humorist Will Rogers drilled a hole at 20th Century–Fox so he could peek into Shirley Temple's dressing room.

Cleopatra earned the Greek nickname She Who Gapes Wide for Ten Thousand Men before she died in 30 B.C.

Richard Pryor's dad died while having sex in the brothel where his mom worked.

Mozart was so inexperienced in sexual affairs that he called in Casanova to serve as a consultant for help on an opera.

Lawrence of Arabia had a thing for being severely beaten by men during his sexual activities.

Both F. Scott Fitzgerald (who liked to have sex in order to warm up for a writing session) and Fyodor Dostoyevsky had a foot fetish; but they had good company. In America alone there are an estimated one and a half million fetishists.

Famous for books that were banned because of their strong sexual content, James Joyce admitted to being turned on by his lover's unwashed underwear.

Clark Gable claimed to have had sex in a canoe, on a fire escape, and in a telephone booth. One of his wives, Carole

Lombard, noted, though, that "to tell the honest truth, he isn't such a helluva good lay."

Benjamin Franklin was a member of the notorious Hellfire sex club and was said to have had a mistress on every street in Paris. Now we know why he's on the hundred-dollar bill.

Anne Frank wrote in her diary, "I go into ecstasies every time I see the naked figure of a woman."

According to Shelley Winters, during the years she roomed with Marilyn Monroe, the sex goddess used to fantasize about having Albert Einstein's baby.

"Plaster casters" were 1960s rock groupies who made plaster molds of their idols' penises. Reportedly, Jimi Hendrix enthusiastically offered his member for immortalizing.

Marilyn Monroe unabashedly claimed to be blonde all over.

Reggie Jackson said that he'd rather hit a baseball than have sex.

Mozart remained a virgin up through his twenty-fifth year because, as he wrote to his father, he had "too much dread and fear of diseases."

* * *

Christian Science founder Mary Baker Eddy lost her virginity at age fifteen and in her eighties suggested that celibacy was the true spiritual condition.

Wilt Chamberlain claims to have had sex with twenty thousand different women. That figures to be two women a day for a little over twenty-seven years.

President Warren G. Harding had sex with his mistress in a closet in the White House.

Movie star Errol Flynn once worked on an Australian sheep ranch, castrating sheep with his teeth.

Marilyn Monroe was paid only $50 for her 1949 nude calendar photo.

Larry Flynt, the founder of *Hustler* magazine, claims to be a born-again Christian thanks to President Carter's sister.

James Dean had a thing for getting beaten and kicked. He specifically liked to have men put out their cigarettes on his chest.

Even though they dated seriously for over a year, John Tesh and Connie Sellecca claim that they refrained from sex because of their religious beliefs.

* * *

Charlie Sheen reportedly spent upwards of $50,000 on the Heidi Fleiss prostitutes.

Along with her affairs with Julius Caesar and Marc Antony, Cleopatra was also married to her brothers Ptolemy XIII and Ptolemy XIV.

According to biographer James Spada, Elvis Presley and Barbra Streisand had a one-night stand in 1969 in Las Vegas.

Stutterer Lewis Carroll would find his speech impediment completely gone when in the company of prepubescent girls, especially the Alice for whom he wrote his *Adventures in Wonderland*.

President Kennedy reportedly told British prime minister Harold Macmillan that if he didn't have nonmarital sex at least once a day he got a headache.

Marilyn Monroe made no bones about the fact that she went pantyless on and off the set.

King Richard I was not only lion-hearted but also gay.

Even though a blood test proved that Charlie Chaplin wasn't the father, a jury forced him to pay child support anyway in a famous paternity suit in order to punish him for his penchant for deflowering young girls.

Before becoming the country's president, JFK was known in Palm Beach as Mattress Jack.

8 Sex in History

Sex has always been a popular subject, ever since the first man and woman (not to mention the first locker-room). Following are some of the more interesting tidbits regarding our carnal past.

The Ramses brand condom is named after the great pharaoh Ramses II, who fathered over 160 children.

In 1860 New Orleans, a bordello would provide a client with a virgin for $800.

Military outposts along the expanse of the Great Wall of China during the Ming dynasty (1368–1644) included a barracks brothel. In addition to their regular duties, government prostitutes were trained as reserve soldiers in the event of an attack by Mongolian hordes.

Depilation, the shaving or removing of pubic hair, was a common practice in Rome, the Middle East, Japan, China, and India, as well as North America. Since the age of sexual initiation in many of these countries was before the onset of puberty, historians believe that many people had become conditioned to bald genitals.

In 1930 there was a nude indoor bicycling race in Paris in which each woman's goal was to be the first to orgasm from rubbing on the seat.

The Roman emperor Nero used to dress up young boys in his dead wife's clothes and then make love to them.

The first mastectomies (breast reduction or removal) were performed in 1671 in England for women with breasts of "prodigious bigness."

The fifth-century B.C. Greek symposium was in actuality an orgy (or at least it led up to one).

The homosexual meaning of the word "fag," which originally was used to describe a cigarette, came from the early-1900s belief that smoking was effeminate.

* * *

The Athenian legislator Solon, in the sixth century B.C., decreed that all husbands must have intercourse with their wives at least three times a month. The reason for legally motivating marital relations was that wives weren't considered desirable sex partners, only childbearers, and most men preferred to find delight in slaves, concubines, or young boys.

The Egyptian *Book of the Dead* (parts of which were written before 2000 B.C.) contains the first known written condemnation of masturbation.

Saint Thomas Aquinas changed the thirteenth-century Catholic attitude toward sex by stating that the sex organs were for procreation only.

Medieval husbands thought that the drinking of holy water would prove whether their wives had been adulterous or not.

It was common in some African tribes to give vasectomies to every male save the chief's eldest son.

In the eighteenth century, another term for anal sex was "to navigate the windward passage."

Nowadays, some prefer love notes while others opt for candy, but in ancient Siberia it was customary for a woman who was interested in a man, and wanted it to be known to him that she was available, to throw freshly killed lice at him.

In 1529, Cardinal Wolsey was accused of giving Henry VIII syphilis by whispering in his ear.

Christianity hasn't always thrown a wet blanket on prostitution, as church-controlled brothels were not uncommon in medieval Europe. One of the first such brothels, named *abbaye,* or "abbey," was restricted to Christians, and its female residents were required to observe the hours of prayer and regularly attend religious services.

Sixth-century A.D. Byzantine emperor Justinian's wife, Theodora, had performed as a striptease dancer and would entertain thousands by having geese peck seeds from her genitals.

The world's first testicle transplant was performed in Saint Louis in 1977. Betcha didn't even know they did them.

The Victorians believed that a woman who was sexually neglected by her husband would get shriveled breasts.

The ancient Egyptians referred to venereal disease as "copulation sickness."

Of all the various "sexual perversions" throughout history,

the most widely condemned has been masturbation.

Mesopotamian kings considered that their "right of the first night"—that is, the duty of deflowering a virgin bride to ensure communal fertility—such an egregious task that they actually charged the groom-to-be a fee to perform the ritual, and those who couldn't pay were forbidden to marry.

It was common in the 1400s in Venice to encourage young men to seek prostitutes in order to guard against homosexuality.

It was a widely held belief during the Middle Ages that both men and women produced sperm.

Native American Caribs had a custom that the wedding of one chief required him to share his bride with all the other chiefs invited to attend the ceremony.

In India, a pagan priest would walk naked through the streets beckoning the faithful to caress his sacred penis.

Pope Innocent VIII was called "the Honest" for admitting that he'd fathered illegitimate children during his papacy.

Cereal legend Dr. John Harvey Kellogg not only was celibate, despite being married, but also strongly advocated abstinence to ensure good health. Also tops on his list of no-no's was masturbation. Thankfully, he wrote a book detailing the thirty-nine signs for detection of "the secret vice of self-abuse," which included having round shoulders, eating clay, and having acne.

By 1906, the practice of removing the ovaries was so popular in making wives more "tractable, orderly, industrious, and cleanly" that it's estimated some 150,000 went under the knife.

While nakedness was considered commonplace to the ancient Greeks, a man was considered indecent if he had an erection exposed.

The feast of Lupercalia, an ancient Roman celebration held every February 15 in dedication to the fertility god Lupercus and the goddess of love, Venus, featured a lottery where eligible bachelors could draw, for a large sum, the name of a young maiden to do with as he wished for the next year.

Valentine's Day is said to have evolved from this ancient Roman feast day.

The ancient Egyptians held that uncircumcised men were barbarians, while the fifth-century Greeks felt the same way about those who had been circumcised.

Thanks to a successful sex-change operation, Michael Clark

was the first person to serve as both a male and a female in the armed forces.

Sixth-century B.C. Athenian legislator Solon passed a law that let dads sell their fornicating daughters into slavery.

Still, Solon didn't have much problem with the fornicating fathers, as he instituted the state-controlled brothel. Not only did legalized brothels include both male homosexual and heterosexual establishments; the fees for the services offered were government regulated.

Proving that sex has always held mankind's center of attention, in 1955, archaeologists in Corsica discovered phallic monuments of six-to-ten-feet-high penises, dating all the way back to the Bronze Age (circa 4000 B.C.).

Men haven't always bragged about the size of their penis; ancient Greeks reportedly admired the small penis and felt larger members were ugly.

It was Aristotle (perhaps making up for his own shortcomings) who first said that a small penis was more fertile, as the sperm had less distance to travel. Of course, he also believed that a woman became pregnant when semen combined with menstrual blood, that being her most fertile time.

It was a custom for members of early religious sects to sleep platonically with beautiful women to prove their convictions.

Harems existed as early as 3000 B.C., and many Persian harems during the seventh and eighth centuries had as many as four thousand females.

During the mid-1800s, statistics show, there were approximately six thousand brothels and eighty to a hundred thousand prostitutes working in metropolitan London alone.

In ancient Rome, bestiality, like today's modern boxing matches, was a public sporting event.

In 1300 B.C., King Menephita returned to Egypt with a collection of thirteen thousand battle souvenirs: the severed penises of vanquished foes.

Chastity belts were still being sold in medical catalogues as recently as the 1930s.

The word "jazz" is believed to have originated as slang for "sex" in nineteenth-century New Orleans, a place that also was popular for that type of music.

The infamous Siamese twins Chang and Eng Bunker not only married (to the Yates sisters) but also fathered twenty-two children between the two of them.

* * *

Pederasty (adult men with boys) is the most common sexual practice depicted on ancient Greek pottery.

Thinking modesty was more important than fine art, eighteenth-century families commonly adapted the portraits of their bosomy seventeenth-century relatives by painting bibs over their exposed breasts.

In the eighteenth century it was common to refer to a penis as a "whore pipe."

In early-sixteenth-century Europe, harlots and courtesans were referred to as "nuns," and a brothel was a "nunnery." The expression "Get thee to a nunnery" was actually an encouragement to go to a brothel.

Now that's hospitality . . . In ancient Phoenicia, a household's daughters were offered as gifts to male house guests.

In 1894, Thomas Edison invented the first peep show machine.

Catherine the Great was into foot tickling and bottom slapping, but was not killed during any escapades with a horse, despite legend.

In England between the thirteenth and fifteenth centuries,

the word "girl" didn't refer to a prepubescent woman but was applied to a youth of either sex.

Victorian mores rose to new heights of prudishness when table skirts were used specifically to cover the table legs, considered sexually suggestive.

A religious movement during the Middle Ages known as Catharism forbade marital sex, feeling that abstinence was the only road to spiritual enlightenment.

While her Roman emperor husband, Claudius, was away, Valeria Messalina turned his palace bedroom into a brothel, charging the male public she serviced the standard legal fee. She also challenged a popular Roman prostitute to a contest to see who could have the most sessions within a twenty-four-hour period. Pliny the Elder proclaimed Messalina the winner; she had bested the competition *by twenty-five men.*

So much for sexually repressed nuns . . . To repel their would-be Scandinavian rapists, the nuns of a convent in Coldingham, Scotland, in 870 A.D. cut off their noses and upper lips. Word has it that it actually worked.

Those trusty English knights during the first Crusade spent their entire campaign fund on prostitutes.

The original sanitary napkin was made from cellulose and

was used as a surgical compress, but quickly was adopted by the nurses for other things because of its superior absorbency.

The expression "Peeping Tom" was originally coined because of the boy who peeked as a naked Lady Godiva rode by on her horse, with only her hair to cover her.

The oldest sexual taboo is incest. However, it was commonly broken by various ancient rulers, from Egypt to Peru, to emphasize their superhuman and divine status, which allowed them to deliberately break it.

Pope John XII used the Basilica of Saint John Lateran (the first-ranking church of the Roman Catholic Church) as a brothel. He died suddenly while engaged in adultery.

It was common at most Greek games for the participants to be completely nude.

In Victorian times, a woman who was "poorly adorned" was small or flat chested.

In the 1800s, the Oneida community in the state of New York gave each man marital privileges with every woman.

In early Christianity, newlywed couples had to wait three nights before they could consummate their marriage. After the "Tobias nights" were over (the term derives from the deuterocanonical Book of Tobit, which tells the exploits of a pious Jew), they also couldn't enter the church for thirty days.

In ancient Greece, women would expose their genitals in hopes of warding off hail, wind, and storms at sea (but obviously not men).

In 1867, it was suggested that women who worked with sewing machines use anesthetic drugs in order to avoid sexual arousal from the vibrating machines.

During World War I, condoms were standard G.I. fraternization equipment.

Apparently more than willing to revel in their sexuality, during the Tudor period (1485–1603) men would wear a *braquette* (codpiece), which made a conspicuous bulge in the pants by simulating an erection.

A hotbed of religion and sexuality, ancient Babylon required that all women serve as prostitutes at the temple before getting married. Historians report that unattractive women had to sometimes serve three to four years before finally being chosen.

The Tang dynasty empress Wu Hou (who ruled 683–705 A.D.)

insisted that all visiting dignitaries perform oral sex on her to pay her homage.

Not one to take adultery too lightly, the Russian czar Peter I forced his wife, Catherine, to watch her lover's execution, then had his head pickled in spirits and kept in the bedroom. While he didn't hold himself to the same high moral standards, he did expect his mistresses to. One who proved unfaithful to him had her head meet the same fate.

The expression "get laid" supposedly has its roots in the Everleigh bordello in Chicago ("I'm going to get Everleighed tonight").

Pope Alexander VI, during one of his many orgies, had fifty prostitutes service the male party-goers, with a prize given to the one with the most stamina. Now *that's* a religious experience.

One may erroneously think that sexual graffiti are a relatively modern phenomenon, but excavations of the volcanic ruins of Pompeii, which date back to the first century, have such obscene comments as *Hic ego puellas multas futui* ("Here I fucked many girls") and *Si qui futuere volet, Atticen quaerat a XVI* ("If you want to fuck, see Attica at No. 16"). Though this sounds a bit far-fetched, keep in mind that a winged penis was the city symbol.

* * *

Napoleon's sister Pauline was infamous for her nymphomania, especially regarding the well endowed. In fact, her doctor implored her to end a yearlong relationship with an Italian painter to alleviate her "vaginal distress."

Many anthropologists feel that the reason early humans lost much of their body fur was the inconvenience it caused during missionary-position sex. Less friction meant more sex.
It was believed that the fierce women warriors called Amazons burned off their breasts as young girls in order to better use a bow and arrow. Hence the name "Amazon," which means "breastless" in Greek.

It is said that Casanova ate fifty oysters for breakfast.

In earlier times, proof of virginity on a wedding night was paramount. As proof, the morning after the consummation, the bloodstained bedsheet would be hung out for relatives and neighbors to witness.

In 1834, Graham not only invented the famous cracker but also insisted that each ejaculation shortened one's life span.

During the Middle Ages menstruating women didn't exactly have it easy. Not only had no one ever heard of Tampax, but afflicted women weren't allowed to go to church or handle meat and other foods (for fear of contamination). In ancient Babylon it was felt that a menstruating woman contaminated everything she touched (including men).

Adolf Hitler ordered that if any movie featured a female character who broke up a marriage, that character had to die by the end of the film.

Men working out at the local gymnasium in ancient Greece always faced the probability of injury to certain areas of the body, especially considering that they got buff by working out in the buff. To help minimize the risk, men would tie the foreskin over the glans of the penis with a *kynodesmē,* or "dog tie."

Those conservative Victorians believed that excessive use of coitus interruptus (pulling out before ejaculation) would cause impotence (at least, that's probably what the guys kept telling their lovers).

The word "frigging" is derived from the Middle English word *fryggen,* "to wriggle," which described masturbation.

The Jewish Mishnah suggests that an unemployed person render his wife her marital due at least once a day as he doesn't have any excuses for being too tired from work.

The Christian polemicist Tertullian (late second century) felt that a person was created at the moment of ejaculation, which would explain why he felt swallowing during fellatio was cannibalism.

The 1930s public enemy number 1, John Dillinger, is reported to have his twenty-inch penis forever preserved in the Smithsonian Institute (it's considerably smaller now).

Supreme Court justice Oliver Wendell Holmes said that comedy could not be obscene because "if anything is funny it cannot be lewd."

Seventeenth-century abortionists openly advertised their services in popularly read newspapers and periodicals under the guise of treating "private disorders of the female" or offering help for "monthly blockage" and "female suppression." A mail-order pill business thrived during this period, dispensing "abortifacients," which were combinations of botanical extracts known to be strong purgatives, such as black cohosh, hemlock, ergot, and snakeroot.

Plymouth, Massachusetts, wasn't just a colony for sexually repressed Puritans. The Merry Mount settlement in 1625 became famous for its acceptance of extramarital sex as well as condoning sex with the local Indian population (why do you think they were so merry?).

Oophorectomies, the removing a woman's ovaries, came into vogue in the Victorian 1800s as a means of curing a host of ailments, including irritability, "simple cussedness," and "eating like a plowman."

Like most modern festivities and traditions, the maypole dance was originally part of a fertility festival, the maypole being a phallic symbol.

It was believed in Victorian times that if a woman bathed in fresh strawberries, it'd help shrink flabby breasts.

It is said that the famous prostitute and madam Calamity Jane earned her nickname because of the social disease she inevitably inflicted upon those who had sex with her.

In colonial America, a bundling board was a board that separated a courting couple who found themselves having to share the same bed. If anything will slow down two eager young lovers, it's a board.

In ancient Greece, dildos were in such short supply that women were forced to share one another's.

In 1833, Daniel Webster began editing the Bible so that young women could read it without blushing.

Forming the letter *V* with your index and middle fingers generally has positive connotations nowadays. But originally it was, in Europe, an obscene gesture symbolizing a double phallus and suggesting infidelity. If you made the gesture to a man, you were essentially saying, "Your wife has been cheating on you."

During the Victorian era it was considered improper to have sex on a Sunday.

During darker times, the Catholic confessional was used by priests to recruit women for sex.

Condoms as we now know them didn't appear until the Philadelphia World Exposition in 1878, about forty years after the invention of vulcanized rubber, which helped in the manufacture of a thinner, more sensitive condom. By 1930 more than 317 million condoms were being sold per year.

Ancient Spartans used to dress their wives as young boys in order to be aroused enough to have sex with them.

Achilles, the famous Greek god of Achilles' heel fame, had sex with the Amazon queen Penthesileia, but not before she died.

The Greek goddess of love and sex, Aphrodite (Venus for the Romans), was born from her father's castrated organs, which had fallen into the sea.

A man of God indeed . . . King Solomon at one time had seven hundred wives and three hundred concubines, according to the eleventh chapter of the First Book of Kings.

While you may have guessed that during the time of the witchcraft inquisitions in the 1400s, sex with the devil was punishable by hanging or burning to death at the stake, you may not have known that, according to confessions obtained through various means of torture by the inquisitors, intercourse with the devil was painful, due to his abnormally large organ, and that his semen was ice cold.

When fifty thousand sperm were first discovered swimming around in a microscope in 1677, they were thought to be parasites.

The Russian holy man Rasputin sported a thirteen-inch penis.

The invention of the chastity belt, first known as "the girdle of Venus" or "the Florentine girdle," was said to originate from Homer's *Odyssey,* in which Aphrodite's husband, Hephaistos, forged a girdle as punishment for her marital infidelities.

The Egyptian pharaoh Cheops used income from prostitution, including that from his daughter, whom he pressed into harlotry, to finance the construction of the great pyramid at Giza.

* * *

During pre-Christian times in Europe, it was held that women who failed to kiss under the mistletoe were going to be rendered infertile.

On the India-Burma border, in Dimapur, you can still see the remnants of the thirty giant, twenty-foot-high phalluses and twenty equally large vaginas built in the fifteenth century by the Kacharia tribe.

Moorish baths in the fifteenth century would have women skilled at the art of pulling out clusters of pubic hair in men to induce orgasm.

It was believed in Victorian times that if a man was too sexually active he would use up his fixed supply of semen and become infertile.

It's claimed that the Nasamones of Libya during the fifth century B.C. required the bride to sleep with all the male guests at the wedding party.

In the mid-1900s some European countries were using X rays as a means of voluntary sterilization of women.

In the thirteenth century, if married Christians were not planning on having children, they were forbidden to have sex.

* * *

In seventeenth-century Italy, it wasn't the men who had all the fun. It was quite customary for a husband to provide his wife with a *cicisbeo,* a male escort, confidant, and lover.

Homosexuality remained on the American Psychiatric Association's list of mental illnesses until 1973.

During the fourteenth century, near London, people weren't too discreet about their brothels. Streets on which they stood had such jolly good names as Whore's Nest, Slut's Hole, and Gropecunt Lane.

Fifteenth-century Paris had a few descriptive street names as well, including rue Puits d'Amour (whore's hole lane) and rue Poilecon (hairy cunt lane).

Coincidence, or indicative of something more? During such sexually repressive periods as the early Christian era and the Puritan and Victorian eras, flagellation reached popular heights as a means of sexual gratification.

Anal intercourse is the most popular sexual practice depicted in pre-Columbian art.

The Egyptian dynasty of the Ptolemies practiced marriage between siblings for over three hundred years without any physical or mental defects in their offspring. In fact, Cleopatra was the sixth generation to be born under such conditions, though she was reported to be extremely ugly.

Julius Caesar was mocked as a "queen" because of his affair with a foreign king.

In some Middle Eastern cultures (especially during biblical times), to ensure no animal blood was used to stain the wedding-night sheet, wedding guests would either wait in the next room or actually be present for the consummation to ensure that the bride was indeed a virgin.

In ancient Babylon, to test a suspected adulteress, they'd throw her in a river, and if she lived she was innocent.

The geisha of Japan would not perform fellatio as it was considered demeaning for the cultured to do so. If you wanted such services you'd have to go to the district of Yoshiwara, where the young girls practiced "fluting."

Saint Swithin reportedly proved his ability to resist temptation by sharing his bed with two attractive young virgins.

Talk about your excessive dowry . . . In the Bible, David brought King Saul the foreskins of one hundred Philistines in order to marry Saul's daughter.

And you thought nuns were sexually repressed . . . The French tickler was invented by a Tibetan monk.

* * *

It's been rumored that Catherine the Great employed in her court six testers, female aides whose responsibility was to screen potential lovers for sexual prowess and venereal disease. I guess it beats digging ditches for a living.

In the fifth century B.C., a Corinthian athlete tried to bribe an Olympic games official with fifty top-quality harlots.

In order to fully finance the cost of constructing Saint Peter's Basilica in Rome, there was instituted a church-imposed prostitution tax, whose revenue exceeded even that from the sale of indulgences.

The first transsexual to reassign his gender was Danish artist Andreas Sparrer, who in 1930 became Lili Elbe.

The first successful artificial insemination of a human female was accomplished in the 1780s by Scottish surgeon John Hunter. But that wasn't his only contribution to the sexual sciences. He also studied venereal disease, infecting himself with gonorrhea and syphilis by making small incisions on his penis, then swabbing the cuts with a probe that had been dipped into the lesion of an infected prostitute. His efforts resulted in a syphilitic lesion bearing his name—the hunterian chancre. He died with the mistaken belief that gonorrhea and syphilis were different stages of the same disease.

* * *

In 1967, a presidential commission recommended the repealing of obscenity laws because, they said, obscenity didn't hurt anyone.

In the nineteenth century, chastity belts were sometimes used to prevent masturbation.

In the 1800s it was common for disreputable surgeons from London to New Orleans to surgically repair a woman's hymen to pass her off as a (more monetarily valuable) virgin.

In 1949, the United Nations launched a universal campaign for the decriminalization of prostitution.

In Nuremburg in the 1400s, money given to a visiting prostitute for her services was tax deductible.

How do you think he became so passive? In 1946, Mahatma Gandhi confessed to taking naked girls to bed with him.

In 1727, Helen Morrison was institutionalized for placing a lonely hearts ad in a newspaper.

It wasn't until September 12, 1933, that gynecologist Dr. Earle Cleveland Haas received a patent for the now-standard internally worn tampon. He dubbed it "Tampax" by combining the words "tampon" and "vaginal pack."

* * *

Attila, king of the Huns and called by some the Scourge of God because of his ferocity and many conquests, died while having sex.

In the Middle Ages, the word "brothel" actually referred to an individual prostitute.

In 1944, pinup pictures were censored to protect the armed forces from depravity (that is, other than killing).

In 1709 it was believed that the widespread infertility of Spanish women was due to singing during sex.

In the 1950s it was the general consensus that eighteen was the peak marriage age.

In 1672 a woman being shipped to populate the colonies was worth 120 pounds of tobacco.

It was customary to keep Egyptian embalmers from the body several days after death to ensure that the embalmers wouldn't try to have sex with the bodies.

In medieval times, it was believed that a virgin's thighbone or elbow mixed into the mortar of a fortress would protect it from falling into enemy hands—and if the fortress did fall, that proved the bones weren't from a virgin. Some believed that London Bridge fell down because the virgin used was not really a virgin.

In fifteenth-century Venice, the government ordered prostitutes to go topless.

There were so many prostitutes selling their wares in early-nineteenth-century Vienna that the ratio was roughly one whore for every eight adult men. On the downside, this not being the era of safe sex, between six and seven thousand women were hospitalized annually with venereal disease.

The Romans were the first ancient society to open a legal chain of brothels.

Physicians in sixteenth-century France, perhaps feeling that they'd missed something the first time around, revived the practice of pulling out pubic hair to cure hysteria in women.

Orgies were originally religious events, being offerings to the gods.

Mistletoe was sexually sacred to the Druids.

Ancient Chinese Taoists believed that immortality could be achieved by having sex with twenty different women each day.

In the mid-1800s, the Perfectionists were founded in Oneida, New York, and practiced a form of communal group sex and child rearing. All members of the group were heterosexually available to one another, though no one was allowed to have children until selected by committee.

Because of her being born on the island of Lesbos, followers of the poet Sappho were called Lesbians. Legend holds that she leapt to her death because of her unrequited love for a young boatman named Phoan.

According to ancient Babylonian law, husbands could use their wives as collateral to get a loan. And just like today, if the loan went unpaid, the collateral was confiscated.

Benito Mussolini would ward off the evil eye by touching his testicle.

Aphrodite was actually the Greek goddess of sexual intercourse; saying she was the goddess of love was putting it euphemistically.

Both Hitler and Napoleon were missing one testicle, proving once and for all that lacking such a measure of masculinity is not necessarily an indicator of a man's mettle.

9 Around the World

Many in the West think that our sexual lifestyle is the universal norm. This from a culture that outlaws paying for sex yet legalizes the buying of drugs. However, there are plenty of cultures that are considerably more uptight, feeling that sex for pleasure is obscene. And on the other end of the spectrum we have societies that don't even have a word for "obscene" in their vocabulary, as there simply are no sexual taboos. In this chapter we take a look at some of the more fascinating facts regarding the sexual habits of our fellow global inhabitants.

In India at one time, a fiancé was required to deflower his future bride if she died before the wedding. The girl could not be cremated until this ritual was carried out in front of the village priest.

According to one Hindu sex manual, those men cursed with a long penis will be wretchedly poor.

Arabs believe that it is a fatal poison to have sex with any woman older than themselves.

On the morning of a bullfight, bulls' testicles are served on rounds of dry toast in celebration of the inspection of the bulls.

The Toda society in India has no word for "adultery" in its language, as the practice is considered socially acceptable.

The Siriono in Bolivia commonly have sex outdoors every afternoon.

In many Ugandan tribes, a king would be insulted if he was offered a virgin bride, hymen intact. She was by law deflowered by proxy, which made her virginity all the purer.

The Masai of Africa, on the other hand, feel that if they have sex during the day, the man's blood will flow into the woman's womb, leaving only water in his veins. Subsequently, they have sex only at night.

* * *

On the opposite end of the spectrum, the nomadic Chenchu tribe of Hyderabad, India, prefer daylight sex, as they fear a child conceived during the night will be blind.

The penises of the Bushmen of the Kalahari Desert are semi-erect at all times.

The next time you're invited to the dinner party of a North African Siwa man, keep this in mind: they feel that a woman will find him irresistible if he secretly laces her food with his semen.

The children of the African Ila are encouraged to fully explore every variation of sexual expression. It's said that as a result there are no virgins of either sex older than age ten in this society.

There are over 114 million women in Africa today who've undergone circumcision.

The Hottentots of southern Africa are so convinced that giving birth to twins is bad luck that they cut off one of the father's testicles before he can conceive.

The Gond tribe of the central provinces in India fear that having sex indoors, where valuables are kept, will anger the goddess of wealth, which explains their preference for sex outdoors.

* * *

Inhabitants of Inis Beag off the Irish coast are truly sexually repressed. The sexes are segregated their entire lives and intercourse is brief and perfunctory, serving only to procreate. Few, if any, even know of the female orgasm.

The Jivaro of South America forbid intercourse for several days following the death of a close family member.

While some here think they're being considerate if they use ribbed condoms, the men in some Southeast Asian villages have a different take on increasing the woman's sexual pleasure. They insert small gold or silver nuggets under the epidermis of the penis via an incision.

In a similar vein, some men in regions of the Philippines and Borneo use an *ampalling* to increase their partner's pleasure. First a hole is cut into the penis and kept open by insertion of a dove feather covered with oil. After healing has occurred, a two-inch rod of ivory and gold is inserted into the hole just before sex. The top of this rod has a knob that is left exposed and used for sexual stimulation of the female.

Burmese men are said to sometimes insert tiny bells into their penises, which make a tinkling sound when they walk.

In Somalia, 98 percent of all women undergo or have undergone circumcision.

* * *

The Bimin-Kuskusmin, an agricultural society, maintain separate "male" and "female" crops, which are ritually fertilized with semen and menstrual blood respectively.

Strangely, the males of the island of Tikopia, near the Solomons, aren't allowed to touch any genitals, even their own. Penetration is handled entirely by the female.

Many societies, such as the Venezuelan Llan Indians, the Brazilian Caingang, and the Bolivian Siriono, permit sexual relations between one's siblings and one's spouse. A husband is allowed intercourse with his wife's sisters, and a wife may have similar sexual access to her husband's brothers.

Women in some Islamic countries may be executed for committing adultery, while men usually get off with what's essentially a hand slapping.

While rear-entry intercourse is the predominate form of copulation for most mammals, there is no known human society where this is the preferred or most prevalent sexual position—which puts even more mystery into the origins of the term "missionary position."

When they reach puberty, boys on the Cook island of Mangaia are introduced to the finer techniques of breast stimulation, cunnilingus, and delayed ejaculation to ensure maximum pleasure for their future partner.

People of the Amazonian Mundurucú tribe refer to intercourse as "eating penises."

Males in Thailand are offered free vasectomies on the king's birthday, which results in lines of over a thousand men showing up for the occasion.

Africans aren't the only modern-day peoples to practice female circumcision. Many Arab cultures such as the Tamin and Sammar also do so. In Asia, Sunna circumcision, or the cutting of part of the clitoris, is practiced by the Moslem population of Java.

In the Weird Puberty Rites file . . . The Poro people of Liberia practice puberty rites in which the circumcised foreskin of the boy is exchanged for the excised clitoris and labia minora of the girl, cooked, and then eaten.

In some parts of Java, couples may have sex in the fields to promote crop growth.

In Ambon, Indonesia, one way of ensuring a bumper clove crop is to have naked men running in the fields yelling, "More cloves," ejaculating all the while.

Americans aren't the only ones with psychosexual hang-ups.

A condition known as *koro,* meaning "shrinking tortoise," occuring almost exclusively in Asian and Oceanic (island) cultures, is characterized by a sudden fear that the penis is shrinking and disappearing into one's abdomen, as well as an overwhelming fear of impending death.

While Western society accepts that frequency of sex usually diminishes after the birth of a child, married couples among the Trobriand Islanders practice abstinence for two years after the birth of a child. Still, this is one year less than the Abipon people practice after a married couple has a child.

While incestuous relationships are prohibited among the general population of most societies, some specific cultures, such as the Azande of Africa, require the high chiefs to marry their own daughters, ensuring the continuation of a royal lineage.

While one wouldn't think it happens a lot, apparently a law has been passed that if a Kurtatchi woman of the Solomon Islands unintentionally reveals her genitals, it can be expected and will be understood if any nearby male sexually assaults her.

Some Native American tribes would send newly menstruating women off to spend years in seclusion as a means of population control.

* * *

The Baganda males have a thing for pendulous breasts, so young women have been known to tie weights to their breasts to make themselves desirable.

Instead of shaking hands as a greeting, the Walibri tribe in central Australia prefer to shake their penises.

In Polynesia, adolescent girls and boys are given sexual technique instruction by an older, experienced person. During this period it's considered perfectly all right to have numerous sexual liaisons, before settling down to married life.

Circumcision rites of the Bala tribe of Zaire once required the excised foreskin of a young boy to be wrapped in a banana leaf and placed on a termite hill to be eaten. The boy's father kept vigil at the spot until all remains were eaten; failure to do otherwise was thought to cause the boy to later become impotent.

Ponapean males are required to have one of their testes removed as part of their puberty rites.

While grooming is considered a type of foreplay leading to intercourse, no kissing, breast stimulation, or caressing prior to copulation is practiced among the Siriono.

Japan's pornographic films are mostly about virginal schoolgirls or new virgin brides giving in to dominant men.

* * *

When visiting another tribe, a Chukchee man of Siberia is permitted to have intercourse with the host's wife. Naturally, if the host should pay back the visit at a later time, the favor is returned.

In some Hindu sects, women without children serve as temple prostitutes in hope of becoming fertile. And just for the record, this temple sex is regarded as a strictly religious experience; there isn't supposed to be any pleasure.

If you think the Western ideal is the only true ideal, consider the South American Siriono. They consider obese females attractive, especially if they have a fatty mons and vulva.

Foreplay is also quite different in other cultures. Prior to intercourse, men and women of the Siriono tribe of eastern Bolivia engage in delousing of their bodies of lice and wood ticks, which are then eaten as a sort of a precopulatory snack.

While an extramarital pregnancy may be a stigma in American culture, among some Oceanic societies, a young unwed girl who becomes pregnant is often considered more desirable as she's proved that she's fertile.

Tupuli is a Cherokee word for the female genitalia and is literally translated as "feathered flying serpent."

* * *

Not your father's salad tongs . . . Samoan marriage rites include the use of a marriage spoon by the bride and groom as they eat. It is actually two half spoons whose handles are carved in the likeness of a naked female and naked male with an erection. The two halves of the spoon fit together in a manner that simulates copulation, forming one large spoon.

As long as it isn't their parents, Lesu children are allowed to watch any adults have sex.

In Tuscany the missionary position is called the "angelic" position.

People seem to have a thing for the evil eye and their genitals. In order to protect themselves from the evil eye, members of the Mambas tribe of New Guinea wrap their penises in many yards of calico.

If a tribe in New Caledonia lost its chief, the entire tribe was expected to abstain from sex for an entire month.

As foreplay a Ponapean man may sometimes put a fish in the woman's vulva and gently lick it.

Anxious to have an affair with a married man? If you practice voodoo, just sew his name into a chicken's bladder.

* * *

Aggressive sex is a way of life amongst the South American Siriono and the Pacific Trobrianders; considerable biting, scratching, and hair pulling occur, escalating as climax approaches.

When the ancient Chinese would have sex with a goose, as a climax they used to pull off its head to feel its death contractions.

Trobriand Islanders of the South Pacific have a thing for biting off their lover's eyelashes and eyebrows during sex.

The Dayaks of Borneo like to insert a metal rod with gold balls hanging from the ends across the top of the penis as a decoration.

Premature ejaculation isn't a problem for the Pacific-dwelling Marquesan men, who've mastered the ability to prolong their erections indefinitely until their female partner has had two or three orgasms.

In order to be legal, porn shops in India are called "museums."

Imagine if men tried to encourage this social change in the West . . . During the final stages of a Hidatsa woman's pregnancy, her husband is allowed to have sexual relations with her sister.

* * *

To produce intense orgasms in women, the Patagonian Indians employ a ringlike device called a *guesquel,* fashioned from the coarse, stiff hair of the mule and fitted around the penis.

The Dani tribe of New Guinea believe that sex is strictly for procreation, not recreation.

The African Hottentots love women with large, fatty buttocks. In fact, their *buttocks* have been known to be as big as two to three feet wide each. So prominent is this feature that it's made its way into medical terminology: the "Hottentot bustle" (excessively fat buttocks) and the "Hottentot apron" (elongated labia minora).

While the Hottentots' condition occurs naturally, young girls of Venda, in the Republic of South Africa, and females of Benin, in western Africa, have to work at it. In order to be considered attractive, they're expected to rub and manipulate their labia to lengthen and enlarge them.

The Ponapeans of the eastern Caroline Islands also like enlarged labias and clitorises. If applying stinging black ants to their genitals fails to produce the desired effect, it's claimed that they'll employ old, impotent men to beat, suck, and pull on the genitals.

Pregnancy's sympathy pains are very real in many South American, African, and Oceanic societies, and expectant fathers experience symptoms of pregnancy so severe that many primitive cultures require a husband to observe a period of confinement during the birth and postpartum phase.

In the United States you send flowers or a box of chocolates, but in many primitive tribes it's still a common practice for the bride's father to deflower her on the wedding night.

Homosexual relationships are an accepted practice among all men and boys of the Siwans of Africa. Those who abstain from anal encounters are thought to be weird.

Australian Aborigines exchange wives as a gesture of friendship and goodwill during ceremonial circumcision rites of puberty.

According to legend, when Burmese women are making beer, they need to avoid having sex or the beer will be bitter.

The vocabulary of Polynesian societies has no words for "obscene," "indecent," or "impure" because they feel sex is never something you should be embarrassed about.

The Chewa of central Africa require entire families to abstain from sex if a family member is sick.

The Zapotec Indians of the Oaxaca Valley think nothing of offering an overnight guest one's wife or unmarried daughter.

Practitioners of the Tantric sect of Hinduism strive to achieve a transcendental state by using specific Tantric yoga positions for intercourse, prolonging the act to the threshold of orgasm without climax or ejaculation, in the belief that higher consciousness can be attained by redirecting the sexual energy of the genitals throughout the body to the brain.

In many cultures, an unmarried woman is considered a virgin, even if she's a prostitute. It's only after marriage that she loses her virginity.

You've got to wonder who comes up with these traditions . . . The Keraki males of New Guinea not only regularly practice sodomy; at puberty all young boys are required to submit to anal and oral sex for a year. After this rite of passage, they're allowed to be involved in this initiation with other newly pubescent boys. The Keraki rationale is that these young boys need to receive mature experienced warrior semen in order to develop into strong men.

Feeling that homosexual anal intercourse could result in pregnancy, the Keraki regularly performed a ceremony in which lime was eaten as a means of contraception. So far, it's worked 100 percent of the time.

A truly Sadie Hawkins society, the Kwoma of New Guinea consider it proper for the girl to make sexual advances rather than the boy, who feels he might upset the girl's parents.

Men are no doubt falling all over themselves in Colombia because if a Goajiro woman is successful in tripping a man during a ceremonial dance, he's required to have intercourse with her.

Western kissing as it's most commonly practiced is not a universal phenomenon. The Tinquian people of the Pacific islands do not kiss, but place their lips close to their partner's lips and rapidly inhale.

The first menstruation of a Bimin-Kuskuman girl involves a ritual requiring the piercing of her nose and left earlobe, and extensive scarification by administration of over one hundred inch-long incisions on her abdomen.

Sumatran men have been known to insert small stones into incisions in their penises to make them more lumpy and pleasurable to women.

When a female member of the Toda in India marries she also becomes wife to her husband's brothers, establishing a sexual relationship with all of them.

Men who serve as pallbearers during a western Caroline Islands funeral are forbidden from having sex for several days.

The Aweikoma of southeastern Brazil use the same term for both eating and intercourse, as both involve entering bodily orifices.

10 Crimes of Passion

Throughout history, sex has had more than its fair share of policing, from laws requiring use of a condom during sex to the custom of castrating the father of an illegitimate child. In this chapter we take a closer look at some of the crimes and misdemeanors involving the most natural of instincts.

While we like to think that we're a fairly open country sexually, the United States has more laws governing sexual behavior than all of the European nations combined. The only legally sanctioned sexual act in the United States is private heterosexual intercourse between married adults.

The Romans would crush a first time rapist's gonads between two stones.

In San Francisco, giving or receiving oral sex is prohibited.

In Florida, having sexual relations with a porcupine is illegal.

In some ancient courts, a husband could demand the complete castration of his wife's lover.

The Asiatic Huns punished convicted male rapists and adulterers with castration. Female adulterers were merely cut in two.

It's illegal to have extramarital sex without a condom in Nevada.

In Harrisburg, Pennsylvania, it's against the law to have sex with a truck driver in a toll booth.

You're forbidden from talking dirty in your wife's ear if you live in Willowdale, Oregon.

There's a law against masturbating while watching two people have sex in a car in Clinton, Oklahoma.

In Washington, it's a crime to have sex with a virgin under

any circumstances, even on the wedding night.

You can't have sex in an ambulance if you're in Tremonton, Utah. In addition to normal charges, the woman's name will be published in the local newspaper. However, the man does not receive any punishment.

Though you may have always wanted to, it's illegal in Newcastle, Wyoming, to have sex in a butcher shop's meat freezer.

If you have the stink of onion, sardines, or garlic on your breath, it's illegal to have sex with your wife in Alexandria, Minnesota.

It's illegal to have sex with a corpse anywhere in the United States.

In Ames, Iowa, you can't drink more than three slugs of beer while lying in bed with a woman.

Fairbanks, Alaska, has a law on the books saying that it's illegal for moose to have sex on the city sidewalks.

Not to be outdone, Kingsville, Texas, forbids pigs to have sex on Kingsville airport property.

Also, in Ventura County, California, cats and dogs desiring to have sex first need to obtain a permit.

The only acceptable sexual position in Washington, D.C., is the missionary position. Anything other than face-to-face is considered illegal.

Adultery laws currently exist in thirty-seven states, with a couple of women recently arrested and convicted on the mere accusation of adultery by their husbands.

States in which heterosexual fellatio, cunnilingus, anal sex, and the use of dildos are illegal (1990): Idaho, Utah, Arizona, Oklahoma, Minnesota, Louisiana, Mississippi, Alabama, Georgia, Florida, South Carolina, North Carolina, Virginia, Maryland, Massachusetts, Rhode Island—and Washington, D.C., as well.

In 1992, England passed a law that makes it illegal to engage in any consensual sex act that would break or bruise the skin.

The vow of a Roman vestal virgin lasted thirty years, and if she engaged in sex before then, she was punished by being buried alive.

An eighteenth-century French prostitute could be spared punishment if she was willing to join the opera.

* * *

Believe it or not, in June 1990 three Connecticut residents were arrested in two separate incidents and charged with adultery, a misdemeanor crime punishable by a maximum sentence of one year in prison and a $1,000 fine.

During the Middle Ages, if you were guilty of bestiality you'd be burned at the stake, along with the other party to your crime.

In 1790 London, the punishment for illegitimate fathers was castration by the local butcher.

During the Renaissance, painters were allowed to paint nudes as long as the feet were covered or not shown.

England's King Canute, who reigned from 1016 to 1035, passed a decree that all wives found guilty of adultery were to have their ears and nose cut off.

In 100 A.D., the Teutons, a Germanic tribe, would punish anyone caught as a prostitute by suffocating them in excrement.

Taking the act of adultery to even more painful heights, the Serni of Brazil take a guilty wife, whip her, and then expose the wounds to fire ants.

The early Christian church forbade couples from having sex

on Wednesdays, Fridays, and, of course, Sundays.

In nineteenth-century Europe, it was okay for female stage performers to show *any* part of their bodies but their toes; that was considered indecent exposure.

The Phoenician princess Jezebel would behead any virgin who didn't submit to her deflowering rites.

In ancient Rome, anyone caught having sex with an animal had to pay a head tax.

To discourage prostitution, King Louis XIV of France would have a prostitute's nose and ears cut off.

Premarital sex is allowed by the inhabitants of Tonga if the girl's parents give their permission and it's understood that she won't get pregnant. If somehow their methods of contraception fail, the couple have to parade around the village naked for several days and apply a magic potion to the fence surrounding the community to prevent disease.

Any man who rapes a dog in Bangkok is charged with cruelty to animals.

In China, masturbation is condemned because it "saps the revolutionary will."

* * *

A man found guilty of violating a virgin in Kafa (in southwestern Ethiopia) may at best find himself without hands, and at worst find himself without a head.

In Crakow, Poland, not only is it a crime to have sex with animals, but three-time offenders are shot in the head.

It's a sin and a crime to have sex with any male animal in Lebanon. However, it's perfectly okay to have sex with female animals.

Six thousand years ago, Egyptians, the first to punish sex crimes with castration, would completely castrate a male convicted of rape. A woman found guilty of adultery would find herself without a nose, the thinking being that without a nose, it'd be harder for her to find someone to share in her adulterous ways.

In London, it's illegal to have sex on a parked motorcycle.

During the 1600s in Massachusetts, a teenage boy was executed for confessing to having had sex with two horses, two cows, and four sheep.

In Middle Eastern Islamic countries, it's a sin and a crime to eat a lamb that you've had sex with.

It's against the law for men to have sex with an alpaca in Peru.

* * *

In Saudi Arabia, adultery is a capital offense punishable by death by stoning.

In the days of Cortés, the punishment for homosexuality or transvestism was death.

The Roman emperor Tiberius forbade the execution of virgins.

Some of the laws that are strictly enforced for those areas that allow prostitution in Nevada are

Women cannot leave their house of employment on Sunday.

They cannot enter a bar, casino, or residential area.

They cannot leave the house between the hours of 6 P.M. and 10 A.M.

No more than three prostitutes may visit town at the same time.

There is a law on the books in rural China that forbids a man to look at the bare feet of another man's wife. He may look at any other part, including her completely nude body, as long as he doesn't see her feet. If he does so much as catch a glimpse of her toes, the offended husband has to kill him.

Thinking that it spread disease, King Henry VI banned kissing in England in 1439.

* * *

Up until 1884, a Victorian-era woman could be sent to prison for denying a husband sex.

Believe it or not, many states have laws prohibiting the mating of horses, sheep, or pigs within a certain distance of a school, church, or residential area.

While their punishment for adultery was not as final as the ancient Israelite practice of stoning, Greek men still had their fair share of discomfort when their pubic hair was removed and a large radish was shoved up their rectum.

You really have to watch yourself if you're a woman of the Mehinaku Indian tribe of central Brazil. If you're foolish enough to enter the sacred men's house, you'll be taken to the woods and gang raped.

11 Sexual Healing

If as much research went into the space program as has gone into sex, we'd have a Starbucks on every street corner on Mars. Ever since man has felt that need, he's been trying to come up with ways to cure impotence and to prevent pregnancy, as well as the many other dangers associated with sex. As this chapter reveals, while our forefathers weren't exactly expanding the frontiers of modern medicine, they should get extra credit for creativity.

To pine for the good old days of medicine . . . A mid-nineteenth-century treatment for cervical and uterine inflammation included the application of eight to ten leeches, via a speculum, onto the cervix, a procedure also thought to induce miscarriage of an unwanted pregnancy. There were plenty of complications arising when a leech would accidentally creep into the uterus.

In ancient Babylon, eating the heart of a beheaded male partridge was considered a cure for impotence.

During the early part of this century, it was believed that masturbation caused insanity, and castration was commonly used as a means of curing those with mental disorders.

To help combat impotence, in ancient Rome it was common for a man to ingest deer sperm or mandrake root (guess which one I would've picked).

While not exactly an antibiotic, mercury was a favorite nineteenth-century treatment for syphilis. It's side effects included bad breath, purple gums, and sometimes death.

Ever on the watch for potential trustworthy birth control options, twelfth-century women were encouraged by some to eat bees.

An ancient cervical cap was devised by the sixth-century Greek physician Aetius, who recommended cutting a pomegranate in half and, after scooping out the flesh, inserting it into the vagina prior to intercourse.

* * *

One "scientific" method of testing whether an Egyptian woman was pregnant was to have her urinate on a cloth bag of wheat and barley. If the seeds sprouted, she was expecting.

Do you cringe at the thought of a vasectomy? Just be glad you weren't a patient of Dr. Weinhold, in the 1920s, who infibulated unmarried males as a method of contraception and also as a deterrent to masturbation. The procedure consisted of piercing the foreskin with a thin wire, then soldering the ends together. They were then left intact until marriage.

In 1899, 176 men in the Indiana Reformatory asked for vasectomies in hope of it curbing their habit of masturbating.

Blame it on the Swiss . . . It was physician S. Tissot (1728–97) who was responsible for promoting the belief that masturbation caused nerve damage and insanity by forcing blood to rush to the head.

If you think that aphrodisiacs such as oysters and Spanish fly are questionable, try this recipe for love on for size. In the early Middle Ages some held that to arouse a man's sexual desire, the wife merely had to coat her naked body with honey, roll in a pile of wheat, carefully remove the grains from the skin, then mill them counterclockwise. The dough was then kneaded between the upper thighs and genitals. The finished bread was assured of making a man who ate it a veritable stallion in the sack. If you instead wanted to render said man impotent, you merely followed the same recipe, but you milled the grain clockwise.

To test the fertility of your female friend during the sixteenth-century, you merely inserted a clove of garlic in the vagina. If after twelve hours her breath smelled like garlic, you could rest easy knowing she was as fertile as could be.

According to the *Kama Sutra,* a mixture of camel's milk and honey will keep a man erect night and day.

The first known contraceptive was crocodile dung, used by Egyptians in 2000 B.C. Having failed to yield the desired results, it was replaced soon after with elephant dung.

If you think the above is a bit fishy, what about the medieval contraceptive favorite of placing a fish in the woman's vagina until it was dead, then removed, cooked, and eaten by the husband?

In the 1800s it was a common belief that if the man climaxed first during intercourse, the resultant child would be a girl.

Greek superstition held that a pregnant woman who dined on the testicles and womb of hares would ensure a son.

It was a commonly held belief among nineteenth-century

gynecologists that if a man drank ten cups of coffee a day, he would become impotent.

It used to be believed that a man infected with a genital disease could engage in intercourse with a virgin to cure his affliction without infecting her. Naturally, virgins were quite highly prized for their medicinal uses.

Aristotle believed that the way the wind was blowing while you were engaged in intercourse could determine the sex of your children.

If you're still not convinced women had it rough throughout history, try this sexual bias on for size. The word "hysteria" comes from the Greek *hystera,* meaning "uterus." That's because during the nineteenth century it was believed that hysteria was a strictly female disorder, caused by not having an adequate outlet to deal with repressed sexuality.

To prevent wet dreams, Victorian men would tie a string around their genitals at night.

If the mercury didn't eradicate your syphilis (and you weren't dead yet), there was the less-than-conventional method, in times past, of getting yourself exposed to malaria, in the belief that the high fever that resulted would cure you.

* * *

It was a common belief in the Dark Ages that if a woman held a pebble while making love she wouldn't get pregnant (why do you think they called it the Dark Ages?).

Another popular method of birth control in the Dark Ages was to have the woman spit into a frog's mouth.

In ancient times it was common for men to take the severed penis of a stag and rub it on their own genitals to promote virility.

What is it with the ancients and animal excrement? Greek midwives treated postpartum bleeding by *orally* administering goat's urine and dung.

To ensure the birth of a boy, a pregnant woman in ancient Greece would eat the testicle of a rooster.

It was felt in the mid-1400s that incest performed upon an altar was an effective guard against the plague.

It was once believed that drinking a mixture of ashes and ox urine could cure a man's impotence.

Athenian women rubbed oil of cedar and ointment of lead on their cervix to prevent conception.

During the Victorian era, women had "sick beds" that they

retreated to when menstruating, as it was assumed one should be incapacitated by such an ordeal.

Another method of primitive birth control employed by the ancient Greeks was for the woman to hold her breath, squat, then sneeze.

According to folklore, if you want to cure infertility, rub your body with vinegar and stand in the sun until it dries.

Yet another popular means of birth control in the Dark Ages involved a woman wearing a cat's testicle in a tube across her navel. (When it's all been said and done, you have to wonder about the people who came up with these things.)